D1559785

Arizona's Tree Squirrels

David E. Brown

Published by

ARIZONA GAME & FISH DEPARTMENT
Bud Bristow, Director

A contribution of Federal Aid to Wildlife W-53-R

Cover photo:
Arizona Gray Squirrel, by Robert E. Parker

First Printing 1984
Arizona Game & Fish Department
2222 W. Greenway Road
Phoenix, Arizona 85023

ISBN 0-917563-00-X

Contents

Preface

I ONCE LIVED IN CALIFORNIA in the Santa Clara Valley—the birthplace of Jack London's dog Buck. The valley is now called Silicon Valley and is all electronics factories and residences, but that wasn't so in the 1950s. The valley was then farmland—fruit orchards mostly—and the surrounding hills were grassy and dotted with oaks where not covered in chaparral. Sycamores, walnuts, and the introduced eucalyptus timbered the arroyo margins, and, in the spring, steelhead still came up the small rivers to spawn.

The mountains, foothills, and farmland were private land and posted against entry. No boys were allowed, unless it was to pick fruit or participate in an "organized" activity. The riparian areas, because of a quirk in California law, were, however, a no-man's land, open to nonsupervised exploration. Thus my innate sense of discovery caused me to explore the countryside via the creek bottoms.

In those days a boy and a gun were inseparable and hunting was the basis of natural history discovery. It didn't take me long to realize that tree squirrels were to be found along the creeks—wherever tall trees were close together. These arboreal rodents were the result, I was told, of a derailment in the 1930s. Grain cars returning from the East had tipped over at Saratoga Creek and discharged a transient cargo of fox squirrels and eastern gray squirrels. The valley's numerous walnut and fruit orchards provided food supplies; the creeks supplied homes and cover. Like the 49ers a hundred years earlier, these California immigrants spread out to reside along the streamways.

There was other game in these unkempt and unmanaged corridors. Brush rabbits, valley quail, doves, band-tailed pigeons—even an occasional mallard fell to my Remington .22 and 16 gauge Stevens. It was the tree squirrels, however, that supplied the most sport. Masters at hiding, and using every available cover when spotted, their presence in the bag was due only to their large numbers. Gradually, hunting alone, I learned to know squirrels.

The gray squirrels kept to the highest and densest eucalyptus. They were wary, kept out of shotgun range, and were hard to get. The less cautious and less agile fox squirrels were more cosmopolitan and varied in pelage. Once I killed a black one, the pelt of which adorned my bedroom wall for years. I was surprised to learn that buds and bark were an important part of the diet of both tree squirrels. I had expected only prunes, walnuts, and storable foods.

One day I hiked farther up Saratoga Creek than the bordering farmlands followed. As I entered the mountains, the creek bottom narrowed and a hillside forest of oaks and madrones mingled with the sycamores of the stream banks. Here I met and killed a western gray squirrel. The beautiful silver gray coat of this California native impressed me greatly. That night darkness caught me as I peddled home on my Shelby Flyer. My gun lay across the handlebars and I had difficulty retaining my hold on the feet of a quail, two brush rabbits, and six squirrels—four eastern grays, a fox squirrel, and the prized western gray. I thus learned to appreciate diversity.

As I grew older I moved on to other game. I discovered girls and went to college. Meanwhile, the farmlands gave way to subdivisions; the creeks and arroyos were channeled and sterilized. The squirrels disappeared or became urbanites. I moved to Arizona and my youthful affair with squirrels was all but forgotten.

A number of years passed before our acquaintance was renewed. As Arizona's small game supervisor, I was charged with developing a census technique for the state's principal game squirrel: the tassel-eared squirrel. For some reason, squirrel numbers would fluctuate from abundance one year to scarcity the next.

Nor was it long before I delved into the phenomena of the great variety of other tree squirrels found in Arizona. No other state has more kinds of squirrels. This was most interesting, given the limited areas of Arizona's forests and the fact that two major North American groups—the true gray squirrels and flying squirrels—were lacking.

The more I learned, the more my interest was rekindled. And I was lucky. Southwestern tree squirrels were just beginning to be studied. D. I. Rasmussen and Joe Hall were doing natural history studies of the Kaibab squirrel, John Farentinos was investigating tassel-eared squirrel social behavior, David R. Patton was determining Abert squirrel habitat requirements, Richard L. Golightly was studying the heterothermy of Abert squirrels, and Richard L. Stephenson was working on Abert squirrel food habits and reproduction. These studies, and the findings of earlier investigators such as Edgar A. Mearns, Vernon Bailey, A. H. Trowbridge, Louis L. Lawson, and James O. Keith, guided my efforts.

The haunts and habitats of all squirrel species were visited and analyzed. Hunter reporting boxes were placed at selected sites, and squirrel feet and hunt data were eagerly collected. Several survey methods were attempted before a satisfactory census technique was developed. Together, these census, age, and hunt data provided the means to crack the code of tassel-eared squirrel scarcity and abundance.

Robert Vahle was meanwhile investigating the caching behavior and habitat requirements of Arizona's red squirrels. Much red squirrel data had also been obtained elsewhere, and some had applications to Arizona. That there never had been a study of Arizona's fox squirrels—the Arizona "gray" and the Chiricahua squirrel—was rectified when the Arizona Game and Fish Commission approved a Federal-Aid Program Narrative for Special Tree Squirrel Investigations. This project was essential to the publication of this book.

More than 200 Arizona gray squirrels and seven Chiricahua fox squirrels were collected. What once was game were now specimens. The field and subsequent laboratory work combined to provide a basic understanding of the natural history of our fox squirrels. The Department could now justify its hunting season and management program for all species of tree squirrels.

To compile and share the knowledge gained thus far is the purpose of this book. Although much remains to be learned, enough information is now available to adequately describe and discuss each variety of tree squirrel and its habitat. The information presented on these pages is the result of study and, although open to interpretation, is based on fact. In so doing, perhaps some myths will be dispelled and some erroneous impressions corrected. Hopefully, too, you will appreciate our squirrels and value their forest habitats a little more. The relationships of these animals to their forest environments is truly one of the most interesting stories in the "outdoor library."

Acknowledgments

This book is the result of the efforts of many people. Among those who gave freely of their knowledge were Drs. E. L. Cockrum, John C. Farentinos, Joseph R. Hall, Donald F. Hoffmeister, W. L. Minckley, David R. Patton, and the late D.I. Rasmussen. They, James K. Evans, Rich Glinski, Rick Rice, Donna Patty-Theobald, and John Theobald gathered the data needed to understand the biology of Arizona's squirrels. Of special importance were the many contributions of Richard L. Stephenson, who gave generously of his valuable expertise and assistance. To Louis Lawson, A. H. Trowbridge, James O. Keith, Ronald Kufeld, Paul Webb, and the other earlier squirrel investigators also goes much credit.

Robert K. Barsch, Randy Breland, Bud Bristow, Tom Britt, Tom Clark, Dirk V. Lanning, Gary McGrath, Henry Messing, Pat O'Brien, Juan Romero, Tom Van Devender, Larry Voyles, Rick Wadleigh, Robert K. Weaver, Jim Wegge, Hal Wenthe, and Rob Young collected squirrels or otherwise contributed valuable location data. Dave Daughtry and Todd Pringle processed the photography. The artwork of Matt Alderson and Lauren P.

Kepner greatly enhances the book. Also helpful along the way were Jim Anderson, Jan Barstad, Neil B. Carmony, Dale Jones, Robert Parker, Jordan C. Pederson, John S. Phelps, Bill Roe, Jack States, and Richard L. Todd.

Special thanks go to the reviewers: Sally Antrobus, Richard Golightly, Donald F. Hoffmeister, Lauren P. Kepner, David R. Patton, Robert Barry Spicer, Richard L. Stephenson, Robert Vahle, and Paul M. Webb. Their expertise and comments did much to improve the accuracy and readability of the manuscript.

The cooperation of the following organizations or institutions is gratefully acknowledged: Arizona Public Service, Arizona Historic Society (Arizona State University), The Museum of Northern Arizona, The Nature Conservancy, The University of Arizona (Mammal Collection), Kansas State University, the U.S. Army at Fort Huachuca, the U.S. Park Service, and all offices of the U.S. Forest Service. Lastly, the important administrative support of Paul Webb, Game Branch Supervisor, and Bud Bristow, Arizona Game and Fish Department Director, are recognized and appreciated.

David E. Brown

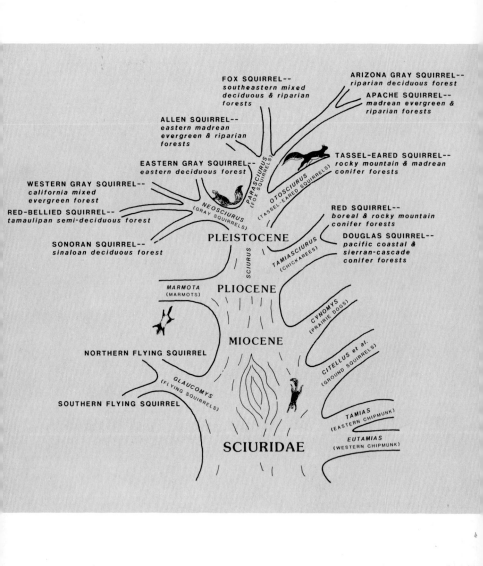

FOX SQUIRREL--
*southeastern mixed
deciduous & riparian
forests*

ARIZONA GRAY SQUIRREL--
riparian deciduous forest

APACHE SQUIRREL--
*madrean evergreen &
riparian forests*

ALLEN SQUIRREL--
*eastern madrean
evergreen & riparian
forests*

EASTERN GRAY SQUIRREL--
eastern deciduous forest

TASSEL-EARED SQUIRREL--
*rocky mountain & madrean
conifer forests*

WESTERN GRAY SQUIRREL--
*california mixed
evergreen forest*

RED-BELLIED SQUIRREL--
tamaulipan semi-deciduous forest

RED SQUIRREL--
*boreal & rocky mountain
conifer forests*

DOUGLAS SQUIRREL--
*pacific coastal &
sierran-cascade
conifer forests*

SONORAN SQUIRREL--
sinaloan deciduous forest

PARASCIURUS
(FOX SQUIRRELS)

OTOSCIURUS
(TASSEL-EARED SQUIRRELS)

NEOSCIURUS
(GRAY SQUIRRELS)

SCIURUS

TAMIASCIURUS
(CHICKAREES)

PLEISTOCENE

PLIOCENE

MARMOTA
(MARMOTS)

CYNOMYS
(PRAIRIE DOGS)

MIOCENE

NORTHERN FLYING SQUIRREL

CITELLUS et al.
(GROUND SQUIRRELS)

GLAUCOMYS
(FLYING SQUIRRELS)

SOUTHERN FLYING SQUIRREL

TAMIAS
(EASTERN CHIPMUNK)

EUTAMIAS
(WESTERN CHIPMUNK)

SCIURIDAE

Introduction

IT IS SOMEWHAT INCONGRUOUS that an arid state like Arizona should possess a great variety of tree squirrels. Within our borders are three races of tassel-eared squirrels, four races of fox squirrels, and two races of red squirrels. This remarkable diversity of native tree squirrels is matched by no other state and is due to the variety and isolation of Arizona's forests.

During the middle of the late Tertiary period about 15–18 million years ago the vegetation of North America consisted of two great forest geofloras: a temperate conifer and mixed deciduous forest in the north, and a broadleafed evergreen tropical forest in the south.[1] As summer rains began to decrease between 14 and 12 million years ago, the forest components of the more northern Arcto-Tertiary Geoflora began segregating out into particular habitats based on moisture requirements. Tropical evergreen forest retreated southward, and a drier broadleaf sclerophyll vegetation (oaks and chaparral) evolved between the two geofloras. By the driest part of the Tertiary, 7 to 5 million

---

[1] For an understanding of the evolution of Southwest forests we are indebted to Daniel I. Axelrod, who has reported extensively on their fossil history.

years ago, this newer Madro-Tertiary Geoflora was centered in what we call "The Southwest" (Fig. 1).

Summer precipitation continued to decrease and winter temperatures became colder. With the advent of the Pleistocene ice ages about 2 million years before the present (ybp), the sorting of Arcto-Tertiary trees accelerated. The cold-adapted and more dry-tolerant conifers survived on upland sites; the deciduous alders, cherries, cottonwoods, box elders, and maples became restricted to wet drainages. The more cold-sensitive sycamores, walnuts, and ash trees gradually became confined to sub-Mogollon streamsides. The newer Madrean forests and woodlands of oak, madrone, and long-needled pines retreated

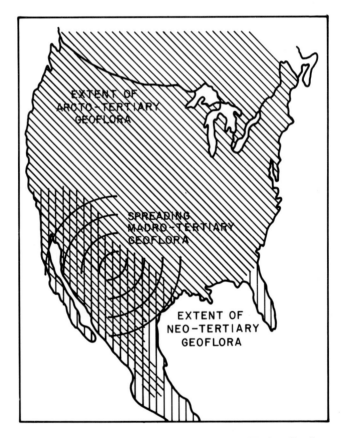

Figure 1. Greatest extent of Arcto-Tertiary and Neo-Tertiary Geofloras and location of the developing Madro-Tertiary Geoflora at the beginning of the Pliocene (5 million ybp).

upslope with increasing aridity, and southward with decreasing winter temperatures. By the end of the Holocene (11,000 ybp) the present general arrangement and composition of our forests had taken shape. Although ice sheets did not reach the Southwest, the colder climates caused by them did; the long glacial periods resulted in the expansion of cold-adapted forests, and the shorter interglacials connected these conifer-clad mountains with corridors of warm temperate Madrean communities.

It was then, during the Quaternary, with the alternating advance and isolation of forests, that our contingent of squirrels adapted to fit their particular forest environments. Actual arrival times of the various species are speculative, as the fossil evidence on this group of animals is meager. No tree squirrels (*Sciurus* or *Tamiasciurus*) have been recorded from Pleistocene deposits in Arizona (Lindsay and Tessman 1974). The historic distribution of today's squirrels was certainly in place, however, by the close of the drier Altithermal, around 4000 ybp, when a new phase of fluctuating wet and dry periods began that has continued to the present (Martin 1970; Fig. 2).

Of the five major groups of North American tree squirrels—tassel-eared squirrels, fox squirrels, gray squirrels, red squirrels, and flying squirrels—three arrived and persisted in Arizona.

Where winter snows were not too deep, stands of ponderosa pine (*Pinus ponderosa*) were inhabited by tassel-eared squirrels. The wetter, but colder, subalpine forests of spruce-fir and mixed conifers were occupied by the red squirrel or "chickaree." The more varied Madrean forests of evergreen oaks, madrones, and pines became the home of the Apache fox squirrel, a form closely related to the eastern fox squirrel. Deciduous forests— Arcto-Tertiary relicts—now greatly reduced in extent and confined to streamways, became the home of the Arizona gray squirrel—a close relative of the Apache fox squirrel that probably arrived from the southeast via Madrean forests and woodland. When and where these forests became isolated, the squirrels were isolated too. Some disjunct forests either were never colonized or, perhaps, upon losing their squirrels with some climatic shift, were too remote for reentry.

The tassel-eared species of squirrels includes the well-known Abert and Kaibab squirrels. These squirrels and their

3

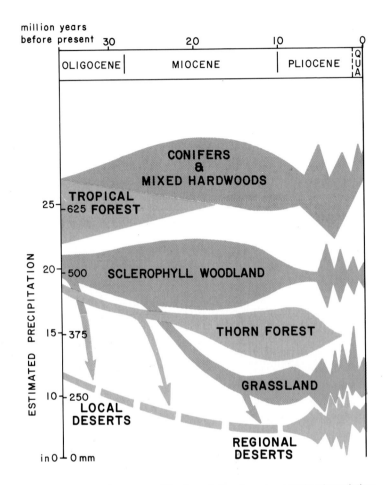

Figure 2. Progressive status of Southwest climate and vegetation through time (pictograph modified from Axelrod 1979). Note the "recent" increasing fluctuation of arid environments.

comparatively recent and dry-adapted Madro-Tertiary ponderosa pine forest habitat are now the most widespread in Arizona. Accordingly, these have been the most studied and are the best known of Arizona's squirrels.

Much more local, but equal to the tassel-eared squirrels in size and sporting qualities, is the Arizona gray squirrel. Because of their restricted distribution to warm Madrean woods and drainage-bound Arcto-Tertiary hardwoods, these animals are less often encountered than the tassel-eared squirrel. The same is true of the closely related Chiricahua fox squirrel—a large

4

russet-orange race of the Apache fox squirrel restricted to the Chiricahua Mountains.

Our smallest squirrel, the diminutive red squirrel, is often abundant within the state's boreal forests—cold-adapted conifers of a modified Arcto-Tertiary forest, now restricted to mountaintops and high plateaus. Commonly called "chickaree," this squirrel is as conspicuous as it is abundant, and unusual indeed is a trip to Arizona's high country without an encounter with this saucy forest dweller.

In the following pages you will meet these squirrels and learn of their habitats, their life histories, and management.

Taxonomy

Taxonomy as used by biologists is the arrangement and classification of plants and animals based on structural similarities. Because an organism's structure depends on its evolutionary history, taxonomy and taxonomic nomenclature should show, or at least reflect, the organism's evolutionary origin, similarity with closely related forms, and how long these forms have been separated from common ancestors.

A hierarchical classification that approximates major steps of evolutionary development was proposed by Carl Linnaeus in his 10th edition of *Systema naturae*, published in 1758—more than 100 years before the concept of evolution had even been formulated! Linnaeus's hierarchy, still in use with minor modifications, is:

Kingdom
Phylum
Class
Order
Family
Genus
Species

These categories have since been added to with Superclass, Subclass, Infraclass, Tribe, etc. (see, e.g., Simpson 1945), but Linnaeus's basic structure and nomenclature remain. The basic building block, or "atom," of the system is the *Species*. Each

5

species has two Latin names—a generic name *(Genus)* for the group of animals to which it belongs, followed by a descriptive name confined to that specific kind of animal. The application of these names follows rigid rules of nomenclature based on precedence.

Each species is composed of potentially interbreeding individuals, reproductively isolated from all other organisms. Reproductive isolation prohibiting interbreeding may result from genetic, size, and/or behavior differences. Subspecies or races are populations or races reproductively isolated only by space or geography, and somehow recognizable from other populations of the species. A Latin modifier after the species name designates a subspecies.

All squirrels are rodents, with large gnawing incisors; i.e., they belong to the Order *Rodentia* of the Class *Mammalia*, and are vertebrates (Phylum *Chordata*) in the Animal Kingdom. Chipmunks, ground squirrels, and tree squirrels are all members of the Family *Sciuridae*, but the tree squirrels belong to a branch of the Family that has opposable hind feet that enable them to rotate the soles of all four feet 180°—like you can do with the palms of your hands. This function enables tree squirrels to run down the trunks of trees, stop, and change direction left or right around the tree, or reverse themselves and climb back up without stopping. Sciurids are all characterized by large bushy tails, short rounded ears, similar-appearing sexes, and seasonally promiscuous reproductive habits.

There are three genera of tree squirrels in North America: *Glaucomys*—the flying squirrels, *Tamiasciurus*—the red and pine squirrels, and *Sciurus*—the gray, fox, and tassel-eared squirrels (Table 1). The three groups of *Sciurus* are differentiated by some taxonomists at the subgenus level as *Parasciurus*, *Neosciurus*, and *Otosciurus*. The skull of gray squirrels *(Parasciurus)* has a longer palate than the other two groups and a peglike premolar anterior to the main premolar; the fox squirrels *(Neosciurus)* have only one upper premolar. Tassel-eared squirrels *(Otosciurus)* differ in having ear tufts and some unique behavioral adaptations.

Of the two species of *Tamiasciurus* (which differ from *Sciurus* in the coiled structure of their reproductive tracts), two races of one species occur in Arizona. Seven races of three

6

Table 1. Taxonomy of the Species and Subspecies of Squirrels in Arizona

Class Rodentia (Rodents)

Family Sciuridae (Tree squirrels, ground squirrels, chipmunks, et al.)

Genus *Sciurus* (Tree Squirrels)

Subgenus *Otosciurus* (Tassel-eared squirrels)

Sciurus aberti (Abert and Kaibab squirrels)

Sciurus aberti aberti (Abert squirrel)

Sciurus aberti chuscensis (Chuska squirrel)

Sciurus aberti kaibabensis (Kaibab squirrel)

Subgenus *Parasciurus* (Fox squirrels)

Sciurus arizonensis (Arizona gray squirrel)

Sciurus arizonensis arizonensis (Arizona gray squirrel)

Sciurus arizonensis catalinae (Catalina Mountains gray squirrel)

Sciurus arizonensis huachuca (Huachuca Mountains gray squirrel)

Sciurus apache (Apache fox squirrel)

Sciurus apache chiricahuae (Chiricahua fox squirrel)

Genus *Tamiasciurus* (Chickarees)

Tamiasciurus hudsonicus (Red squirrel)

Tamiasciurus hudsonicus mogollonensis (Arizona red squirrel)

Tamiasciurus hudsonicus grahamensis (Graham Mountain spruce squirrel)

---

species of *Sciurus* have been described from the state. These include three races of the only species of tassel-eared squirrel *(Sciurus aberti)*, three races of the Arizona gray squirrel *(Sciurus arizonensis)*, and a race of the Apache fox squirrel *(Sciurus apache chiricahuae)*. Both of the latter two species have only one upper premolar and are actually fox squirrels. There are no true gray squirrels in Arizona.

All species of *Tamiasciurus* and *Sciurus* are diurnal, engage in mating chases during the short period the female is in estrus, do not hibernate, and are generally solitary except during the mating season and when the female is raising young. Except for the reproductive organs and a tendency for females to have longer tails, the sexes are similar (= monomorphic). The four Arizona species all have light eye rings, build nests or dreys, and have generally about the same breeding season. Despite these similarities, there is no record of any of the species interbreeding.

"Sciurus Abertii, Woodhouse"

Reproduced from *Report of an Expedition down the Zuni and Colorado Rivers,* by Captain L. Sitgreaves (Washington: Robert Armstong, Public Printer, 1853) Mammals, plate 6.

Tassel-eared Squirrels

Sciurus aberti

THIS ATTRACTIVE SQUIRREL was first described in 1852 by Dr. S. W. Woodhouse from specimens taken on the San Francisco Peaks, Arizona. Woodhouse was then with Captain Sitgreaves on his survey of northern Arizona and named this new species after Col. J. W. Abert, then head of the U.S. Corps of Topographic Engineers and brother-in-law of the illustrious John C. Fremont. Abert had explored the squirrel's eastern range on the east slope of the Rocky Mountains in 1845–46 and perhaps knew of its existence. For whatever reason, the two have been linked together ever since.

If the Kaibab squirrel is considered a race of tassel-eared squirrel, there are six presently recognized sub-species within this group (Hoffmeister and Diersing 1978, Fig. 3). Of these, the Abert squirrel *(Sciurus aberti aberti)*, Chuska squirrel *(S. a. chuscensis*, Goldman 1931a), and Kaibab squirrel *(S. a. kaibabensis*, Merriam 1904a, 1904b) occur in Arizona (Fig. 4). All are restricted to ponderosa pine forests and are geographically isolated.

Description

These are large squirrels. Adults will weight from as light as 16 ounces to between 18.5 and 29 ounces; the average in autumn is about 23 ounces (Keith 1965, Stephenson 1975, Patton et al. 1976). An individual's weight is influenced by physical condition, reproductive status, and amount of stomach contents. Generally, the animals weigh most in autumn and least in late winter and early spring—reflecting their diet and body condition (Stephenson 1975). Females average slightly more than males; Hall (1981) reported a record weight of 2 lb 1.6 ounces for a female Kaibab squirrel taken in August!

Except in midsummer, these squirrels possess tufts or "tassels" of hair extending beyond the tips of their ears—hence the name tassel-eared squirrel (Figs. 5a and 5b). In winter these tufts

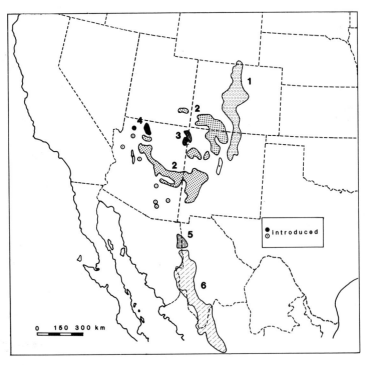

Figure 3. Distribution of the tassel-eared squirrel in North America. **1.** *S. a. ferreus;* **2.** *S. a. aberti;* **3.** *S. a. chuscensis;* **4.** *S. a. kaibabensis;* **5.** *S. a. barberi;* **6.** *S. a. durangi.*

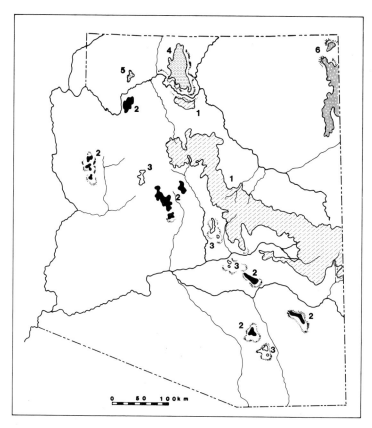

Figure 4. Distribution of tassel-eared squirrels in Arizona, 1980. **1.** *Sciurus aberti aberti*—native population; **2.** *S. a. aberti*—introduced population; **3.** *S. a. aberti*—recent population; **4.** *S. a. kaibabensis*—native population; **5.** *S. a. kaibabensis*—introduced population; **6.** *S. a. chuscensis*—native population.

may exceed 1.5 inches in length, making these squirrels distinctive from any other squirrel in North America. As in all sciurids there is little or no difference between the sexes in measurements or pelage.

Most Abert and Chuska squirrels in Arizona are a peppered iron gray with white underparts; a narrow black lateral stripe separates these colors between the forelegs and hind legs. The gray tail is large, bushy, and fringed in white. There is much white on the feet, and a white eye-ring is conspicuous. A dark russet or chestnut stripe of varying width and length is usually present on the back. Although both individuals and subspecies

Figure 5a. An Abert squirrel in summer pelage in the high Sierra Madre of Mexico. Note the lack of ear tufts and superficial resemblance to the eastern gray squirrel and Arizona gray squirrel. (Photo by Dirk V. Lanning.)

Figure 5b. Portrait of an Abert squirrel with ear tufts prominently displayed. (Photo by Richard L. Stephenson)

vary in this latter characteristic, the back of the ears are always chestnut brown with black, or at least dark, hair tufts. Some populations of *S. a. aberti* in the San Mateo and other mountains in New Mexico, and *S. a. ferreus* in Colorado, have a high incidence of melanism or black pelage (Findley et al. 1975). Farentinos (1972a) found more than half the tassel-eared squirrels in an area in Colorado to be the black phase, as did Ramey and Nash (1976). The Kaibab race has a black belly and a "whitish" tail (Fig. 6). Black-bellied and other melanistic individuals are occassionally found elsewhere above the Mogollon Rim in Arizona (see Mearns 1907), but dark morphs appear less frequently in southern populations. Only the white-bellied, gray phase is known from below the Mogollon Rim and the Sierra Madre Occidental in Mexico—a seeming reversal of Kelker's Rule that boreal populations of a species are more lightly colored than tropic ones.

Behavior. Tassel-eared squirrels are generally solitary or at least nongregarious except during the breeding season and when the young are dependent on their mothers. There is no social structure as is found in prairie dogs (*Cynomys*) and other colonial rodents. The only territorial displays outside the mating season are low-intensity aggressive encounters between animals sharing the same feeding area: tail fluffing and flicking, laid-back ears, and foot stomping—the same actions that are elicited by a human intruder. Aggressive behavior is usually male to male or male to female and is female to male only during mating or pregnancy (Farentinos 1972b).

Because of the lack of social organization, there is no need for complex vocalizations. Except for a number of chirps, growls, screeches, and squeals that are given during mating or when excited, the animals are generally silent (Farentinos 1972b). The most frequently heard vocalization is a squeaky bark or *quirk*, immediately recognizable as belonging to a large squirrel. This is an alarm call, usually given from a tree to announce a real or imagined threat. It may be given singularly or repeated over and over, roughly in relation to the degree of the animal's nervousness and agitation. These calls are most frequently given by threatened females and responding juveniles and are most often heard in autumn.

Figure 6. Portrait of a Kaibab squirrel. Note the dark underparts, white tail, and less defined eye ring.

Tassel-eared squirels are almost entirely diurnal, with activity usually beginning at first light and continuing interruptedly with rest periods until dusk. The animal then retires to one of its sleeping nests for the night. At this time an exception to the animals' normally solitary existence has been observed. Females may share nests for the night with other squirrels—especially one of the young of the previous year (Keith 1965, Farentinos 1972c).

Squirrels have good vision, hearing, and smell. Much of the day is spent foraging, in that the animal stores little, if any, food. When seeking such preferred foods as fungi and mast, as much time may be spent on the ground as in the trees. This is when the squirrel is most likely to be encountered.

Most activity is during the morning on clear, still days; the animal is least active on windy, inclement days, and in the early afternoon. The heat of the afternoon is spent in a nest or on a foliage-shaded limb; conversely, during the cold of winter, much time may be spent basking on a limb in the sun (Golightly and Ohmart 1978). All resting is done in trees. When startled, a tassel-eared squirrel invariably takes to a suitable pine tree. Here it seeks the highest reaches, attempting to conceal itself in the denser branches and needles. A favorite tactic is to then remain immobile until danger passes. Usually 45 minutes or more elapses before the squirrel will move.

If the tree is of insufficient height or possesses inadequate cover to conceal the squirrel, the tree will be abandoned for one more suitable. Leaping from branch to branch, the squirrel displays a fair amount of agility, although nothing to compare with the smaller red squirrel or Eastern gray squirrel (*Sciurus carolinensis*). The tail is used as a balance, and should the distance between trees be too great, causing the squirrel to fall, it will land on its feet, cushioning much of the shock on its chest. Only momentarily stunned, the squirrel then runs off to try another tree.

Food habits. In late April, May, or early June, the staminate flowers of ponderosa pine are green and succulent and are for a short time the tassel-eared squirrel's major food source. These pollen-producing male flowers are abundant for about two weeks each year and consist of clusters of bean-shaped bodies about ½ x ¾ inches when mature (Fig. 7). The number of flowers per cluster varies but are usually between 10 and 20. The squirrels clip the terminal end of the flower-bearing branch along with the crown of developing needles (then about ½ inch or less in length), eat the flowers, and discard the remains.

The female, or ovulate flowers of ponderosa pine also develop into conelets (*strobili*) in late spring. Conelets are not utilized, although tassel-eared squirrels may clip and use conelet-bearing branches to obtain inner bark. When conelets are fertilized the following spring, they begin developing as cones, and are a preferred food. During summer months the squirrels cut and remove the maturing cones, and, after removing the scales, they eat the developing seeds along with the moist surrounding tissue. The cone center, or core, is discarded after feeding. As a rule, all feeding is done in the tree where the cone

Figure 7. Staminate (male) flowers of the ponderosa pine. These high-energy and abundant foods are associated chronologically and probably biologically with the advent of the tassel-eared squirrel's breeding season.

is produced; uneaten cones are rarely dropped to the ground, and few, if any, are buried or cached. A concentration of cone cores and scales invariably indicates the midden of a red squirrel.

The sizes and shapes of the discarded cores indicate the progressive growth of the cones. In early summer the discarded cores are cylinderlike objects as small as ⅜ inch in diameter by 1 inch in length. By early October the cores are triangular shaped and nearly 3.5 inches long, with a width up to 1.5 inches. The scales, except for a few terminal ones, will have been removed and the seeds eaten (Fig. 8). Squirrels do not cut mature cones with expanded scales.

Each mature ponderosa pine normally produces a cone crop annually (the species is monoecious—both male and female flowers occur in the same tree). The number of cones produced is influenced by the size, age, vigor, and even location of the individual tree (Larson and Schubert 1970). Seed production in different years may fluctuate from almost no cones to "bumper crops."

Hypogenous (subterranean) and other fungi associated with pine trees and pine forests are another important food source during summer and early fall (Stephenson 1975, Fig. 9). These mushrooms, particularly "truffles" of the genera *Gautierea*, *Rhizopogon*, and *Morchella* are at least as reliable a food source as pine seed and are probably the most consistently important dietary items.

All through the spring, summer, and early fall, food is usually plentiful and the squirrels gain weight. However, by October or November the above food sources may become scarce or, with the onset of winter snows, largely unavailable. Now the squirrels must rely on inner bark and apical buds—again provided by the ponderosa pine tree.

When feeding on inner bark, tassel-eared squirrels bite off the ends of selected branches. The terminal portion of the removed branch with its cluster of needles is bitten off and allowed to fall to the ground. The squirrel strips off the segment's outer bark and feeds on the inner bark (phloem and xylem). The unconsumed woody portion of the segment is then discarded. This feeding technique is characteristic of tassel-eared squirrels, and

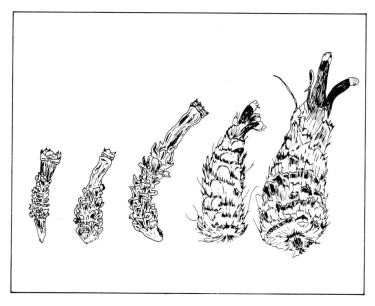

Figure 8. Relative size of cone cores dropped throughout the summer by the tassel-eared squirrel.

"clippings" of terminal needle clusters on the forest floor accompanied by "peeled twig" segments can be used to determine the squirrel's presence (Fig. 10).

Inner bark is low in food value (Patton 1974), and squirrels lose weight when forced to rely entirely on this food source. If the winter is severe and the animals are denied other foods for 60 days or more, their condition deteriorates. Stephenson (1975) found squirrels to lose as much as 25% of their body weight under these conditions. Mange may appear, the animals easily go into shock, and mortality increases.

Buds are eaten directly from the tree; the twigs bearing them are not generally removed (Stephenson 1975). Other food items include dwarf mistletoe berries (*Arceuthobum vaginatum*), insects, various greens, the seeds and inner bark of conifers other than ponderosa pine, and even pine needles. In some areas and in some years, Gambel oak (*Quercus gambeli*) acorns provide an important mast crop.

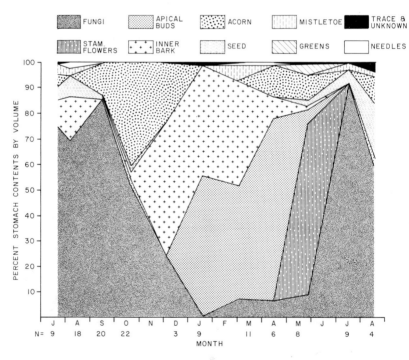

Figure 9. Seasonal food habits of the Abert squirrel on the Mogollon Rim, Arizona, 1972–73: Stephenson 1975.

Figure 10. Clippings and peeled twig feeding detritus of a tassel-eared squirrel. Although other squirrel species may generate clippings. the tassel-eared group of squirrels also discards peeled twig segments (Rasmussen et al. 1975).

Much of the squirrel's habitat is devoid of permanent water, and free water, while taken readily on occasion and when available, does not appear to be a requirement for the squirrel's presence. Presumably the high moisture content of fungi alleviates the need for water during summer when moisture demands would otherwise be high. Some observers, including the author, have observed concentrations of up to 11 squirrels drinking at watering sites during October and November. These observations were during dry periods and prior to the advent of snow, suggesting that the desire for water may have resulted from a dry diet when succulent foods were scarce.

Nests. Tassel-eared squirrels build nests of ponderosa pine boughs. Because pine trees are resistant to rot, hollow trees are scarce; the few den trees that have been found are usually old cavity-prone Gambel oaks (Patton 1975b). An exception occurs in the Sierra Madre Occidental, where Dirk V. Lanning (pers.

comm.) and Jim Shiflett observed Abert squirrels using cavities in pine snags and in quaking aspens *(Populus tremuloides)*. These cavities presumably had been made by woodpeckers *(Colaptes cafer* and others), and the squirrels were vying for their use with thick-billed parrots *(Rhynchopsitta pachyrhyncha)!*

Nests serve as nurseries, as shelter from inclement weather, and are used to sleep in at night as well as for daytime naps. Their insulation properties are important for maintaining thermal regulation, and nests are probably essential for the squirrel's winter survival (see, e.g., Golightly and Ohmart 1978). Each squirrel generally has several nests located at strategic locales within its home range and some nests are used for years (Patton 1975b). Although nests are used and maintained throughout the year, most active nest building takes place in late spring and early summer. This is the time before the young are born and when an abundance of food allows time for home improvements.

The selected nest tree is usually one of a group of trees with interlocking crowns—preferably a tree in the interior of such a group. Such a location allows alternate means of arrival and egress; nests can be entered or left without climbing or descending the nest tree. Hall (1981) observed that squirrels approached and exited nests containing young via alternate trees, and Pederson et al. (1976) found that when all trees adjacent to the nest site were felled, the nest was abandoned.

Nest trees are large "black jack" or "yellow-bellied" pines from 15 to 20 inches diameter at breast height and usually more than 100 years of age (Patton 1975, Pederson et al. 1976, Farentinos 1972c). The nest most often is from 30 to 50 feet above the ground (extremes are 15 to 85 feet) and located about three-fourths of the way up the tree. Nests farther up would be less protected, less concealed, and more subject to wind blow.

Crown densities of the nest tree and surrounding trees are characteristically high, and with a little experience "nest situations" can be readily spotted. Keith (1965), Farentinos (1972c), and others found a preference for nests on the south or southwest side of the tree. Presumably this allows for maximum solar radiation and heat absorbtion, thereby enabling the squirrel to keep as warm as possible during winter.

Nests are constructed almost entirely of terminal pine

branches from 6 to 24 inches long. Leaf nests are virtually unknown. Branches are cut from the tree and carried in the mouth to the nest site—most often at a fork formed by the trunk and a large lateral limb (Fig. 11). Here the cut ends are jammed into branches and arranged to form a crude platform. More cut branches are forced into the started platform until an interwoven mass of twigs and needles forms a ball, or bolus, 12 to 40 inches in diameter; the average bolus is about 18 inches in diameter (Keith 1965, Farentinos 1972c, Patton 1975, Pederson et al. 1976, Hall 1981). Seldom is more than one nest built in the same tree.

The squirrel uses its body to form a hollow about 6 inches in diameter inside the nest. A somewhat narrower entrance connects this interior chamber to the outside. Usually the entrance (sometimes two entrances) is located at or below the center of

Figure 11. Nest of a tassel-eared squirrel. This nest is unusual in that it is in a lone tree and not in a group of pines.

the bolus, and the compact woven roof is relatively rainproof. The inner chamber is then lined with grass, juniper bark, aspen bark, rags, paper tissues, or any other available soft material. Inside the nest one may find, in addition to lining material, bits of bone, pieces of fungi, some fleas, a partially eaten epigeous mushroom, but no cache of food. Feces are almost always deposited outside the nest and never in the inner chamber.

Nest construction takes several days. Work is intermittent, with the squirrel working up to 30 to 45 minutes at a time. Generally nests used for sleeping or resting are of less sturdy construction than those used during winter and for raising young. Nests used as summer resting sites may be merely platforms open at the top. Old, abandoned nests are brown; maintained, active ones are green and blend in with the needle foliage of the tree. Abandoned nests usually disintegrate within two seasons.

Squirrels often use the small abnormal growths of pine twigs resulting from an infection of dwarf mistletoe to start a nest. These prefabricated "broom nests" are usually farther from the main trunk than bolus nests as the squirrel does not initiate the nest site. Farentinos (1972c) found broom nests to be popular and to constitute 25% of all nest sites on his study area in Colorado.

Distribution

Few animals are as closely associated with a single habitat type as are these squirrels; they are found only in the dry ponderosa pine forests of the interior Southwest. Even here they are not universal and are restricted to forests where winter snows are moderate and continuous snow cover generally lasts less than three months. For this reason, tassel-eared squirrels are restricted to mountains and plateaus in Arizona and New Mexico, the eastern front of the Rocky Mountains from New Mexico north to the Wyoming-Colorado border, the San Juan Mountains in Colorado and New Mexico, the Manti-LaSal Mountains in southeast Utah, and the highest reaches of the Sierra Madre Occidental in Chihuahua and Durango, Mexico (Fig. 3).

Tassel-eared squirrels are absent from ponderosa pine forested mountains in the Transverse and Peninsular Ranges in

California, the Sierra-Cascades, and most of the Great Basin. Many small ponderosa clad mountains are also devoid of squirrels; e.g., the Davis and Guadalupe mountains in Texas, the Sacramento Mountains in New Mexico, and the higher mountains in Sonora.

In Arizona, this squirrel was originally confined to the large expanses of ponderosa pine above and below the Mogollon Rim, the high plateaus on the north and south rims of the Grand Canyon, and to the Lukachukai (Chuska) Mountains and Defiance Plateau of the Navajo Indian Reservation. Elevations range from pine stringers as low as 5300–5500 feet along canyons to as high as 9600 or more feet on south slopes adjacent to subalpine forests.

In the 1940s Abert squirrels from Fort Valley Experimental Forest near Flagstaff were traped and transplanted to ponderosa pine forests in the Pinaleño (= Graham), Catalina, Pinal, and Bradshaw mountains, Granite Mountain, Hualapai Mountains, and Hualapai Indian Reservation. An unrecorded transplant also introduced Abert squirrels to Mingus Mountain (Paul Webb, pers. comm.). These introductions were all successful. The squirrels increased and spread rapidly, and these areas now support well-established populations (Fig. 4).

Further introductions to central and southern Arizona were stopped due to concern over the potential for competition and "inbreeding" with endemic species. Although the native squirrels were not extirpated, apprehensions concerning their displacement were not totally without justification. The introduced Abert squirrels increased and demonstrated an ability to disperse widely. The newcomers spread naturally to the Superstition and Rincon mountains, presumably from introduced stock in the Pinal and Catalina mountains. The small pine forests of the Mazatzals southward to Mt. Ord have also recently become colonized without assistance.

Between 1972 and 1977, 21 Kaibab squirrels were transplanted from the Kaibab Plateau to Mt. Logan on the "Arizona Strip." No tree squirrels resided there, and a successful introduction meant that the Kaibab subspecies would not be restricted to one geographic locale. These transplants, too, were successful, and today Kaibab squirrels are present in the limited pine stands of the Sawmill Mountains, Mt. Emma, and Mt. Trumbull (Fig. 4).

The only sizable pine forests in Arizona not now inhabited by tassel-eared squirrels are those in the Pine Mountain Wilderness Area, on Four Peaks in the Mazatzal mountains, and the Santa Rita, Huachuca, and Chiricahua mountains. These ranges all possess native tree squirrels, and futher introductions are not desirable. The distribution of tassel-eared squirrels in Arizona is now greater than at any historic time.

Habitat. To reiterate, the home of this squirrel is ponderosa pine forest. Its ecological relationships and dependence on this tree are well documented (Rasmussen 1941, Keith 1965, Rasmussen et al. 1975, Patton 1975a, Stephenson 1975, Pederson et al. 1976). Where ponderosa pines are lacking, the squirrel is absent. Only once, in a grove of evergreen oaks in Tripp Canyon in the Pinaleño Mountains, have I seen tassel-eared squirrels out of sight of a ponderosa pine. These animals were foraging on the ground for acorns and presumably were ther for only a short time; almost always, tassel-eared squirels are within 20 yards of a good-sized pine.

Within the forest there is much variation in the desirability of the pines for squirrels. Tree characteristics largely determine the quality of squirrel habitat. Originally, ponderosa pine occurred as clumped groups of older age-class trees (Rasmussen 1972). Virgin forests, except where opened by fire or other disturbance, were composed of large trees, more than 200 years old and more than 100 feet tall. Although the tassel-eared squirrel is a climax species adapted to climax forests, the squirrel can do well in managed forests, if certain principles are followed.

Patton (1975a, 1977) described good cover habitat as uneven-aged pine stands composed of small even-aged groups within the stand and containing tree densities of between 200 and 250 trees per acre. Mean tree sizes were between 11 and 13 inches diameter at breast height (dbh), with small groups of large trees to provide a mosaic of height groups. Pederson et al. (1976) considered good squirrel trees also to be from 12 to 19 inches dbh and above 45 feet in height. Large trees greater than 36 inches dbh are the best cone producers, and nest trees are characteristically in groups of 60+ foot trees (Patton 1975a). There is a direct relationship between the number of interlocking crowns and the quality of habitat (Fig. 12).

Figure 12. Good Abert squirrel habitat on the Mogollon Rim in Arizona, June 1972. There are two dominant age classes, one of large mature trees more than 100 years of age with interlocking crowns.

Other forest trees are relatively unimportant to the squirrel (see, e.g., Ratcliff et al. 1975). Mixed conifer forests of Douglas fir *Pseudotsuga menziesii*), white pine *(Pinus strobiformis)*, white fir *(Abies concolor)*, and other conifers are occupied by tassel-eared squirrels only where ponderosa pine is present. White pine cones may even provide an important, if local, food source (Dirk Lanning, pers. comm.). At the lower edge of the pine forest the squirrel disappears as pinyon pine *(Pinus edulis)* or other trees become dominant.

An exception to pine consociations as favored habitat is large Gambel oaks, which periodically provide an important if unreliable supply of mast (Stephenson 1975). The bare understory and needle-mat forest floor characters mentioned by many authors to describe tassel-eared squirrel habitat appear to be features of mature or well-stocked pine forest more than a requirement of the squirrel *per se*. More important is the supply of

25

hypogeous mycorrhiza fungi. These subterranean fungi are an essential component of both squirrel diets and pine forest (Maser et al. 1978).

Life History

The annual cycle of the tassel-eared squirrel is well coordinated with that of its ponderosa pine host. The onset of the squirrel's short breeding season and prenatal period coincides with the pine's production of succulent staminate (= male) flowers (Rasmussen 1972). It appears that these high-energy foods trigger stimuli that put the squirrels in breeding condition; Stephenson (1975) found the mating season was postponed until the arrival of spring and high-quality foods as staminate flowers.

Recruitment. The female is receptive to breeding for only about 18 hours; her mating season is a one-day event that occurs but once each year (Farentinos 1972b). Even then, it appears that all females do not come into estrus every year. Males are sexually active from about the end of April to the end of June, given seasonal and individual variations. Stephenson (1975) found that although testes may reach maximum development as early as January, the accessory sexual organs are not fully functional until high-quality foods are available. There is, therefore, annual variation in reproductive condition, but peak mating activity usually occurs in mid-May (Stephenson 1975).

When Farentinos (1972b) studied Abert squirrel mating behavior in detail, he found that as a female approaches estrus, wandering males and those from adjacent home areas are alerted to the coming event by olfactory cues. Should sniffing males approach too close, however, she promptly attacks them. On the early morning of the peak day of estrus an entourage of males awaits in the vicinity of the female's nest. A mating bout, or chase, then begins in which one male leads (Fig. 13). This dominant, or alpha, male is commonly the one whose home range is closest to the female's. With rare exception, he successfully maintains the favored position behind the female against all rivals—for a while.

There is no courtship. The males follow the female on her

26

rounds through the forest; hence, the term chase. Even now the female is difficult and defends her virtue from the principal suitor. Actual mating takes place in the trees, the female clinging to the trunk or limb while the male clings to her. Copulation is aggressive and hurried, and averages between one and two minutes ($\Sigma = 72$ seconds).

Despite the activity of the dominant male, who invariably copulates first and often, numerous copulations are made by subordinate males. These animals are usually those high on the chase hierarchy, and are actively solicited by the female when the alpha male is repulsing rivals or is otherwise distracted. These lapses increase as the day continues and the fatigue of combat and mating take their toll. Dusk ends the mating bout, with the original dominant male now usually absent.

After a gestation of about 40 days, two to four blind and completely furless young are born; these weigh about 0.4 ounce each and are about 2.4 inches in length (Keith 1965). Although the young may be moved, they do not leave the maternal nest

Figure 13. A mating bout of Abert squirrels captured by wildlife photographer James Tallon at Sunset Crater National Park on June 29, 1981—a late date for such activity. The female is at the top of the snag; the alpha male is directly below her.

until 7 to 9 weeks of age, usually emerging for their first visit to the outside world sometime in August. Growth and development are then rapid, and in about 20 more days the young are weaned and able to fend for themselves. The total dependency period is about 70 days. By now it is usually mid-September; in another week or two the almost-full-grown young have dispersed and the matriarchal family has broken up. There is no time to raise a second family, and reports in the literature of these squirrels having more than one litter per year are in error. Only a month or so remains to accumulate fat reserves and prepare for the coming of winter and hard times.

Population characteristics. Trapped samples of tassel-eared squirrels show a preponderance of males (Keith 1965, Farentinos 1972a, Pederson et al. 1976). Of 853 animals trapped in the above studies, 484, or 56.7%, were males. This imbalance may be at least partially due to trapping bias; Stephenson (1975) obtained 61 males in a sample of 135 animals shot during a year of low population levels—a ratio of 0.82 male per female. Mearns (1907) also collected fewer males than females (12:17). Differential mortality between sexes has been documented for other squirrels and sex ratios may be influenced by population densities and the percentage of young animals in the population (see, e.g., Smith 1968). Until more definitive data are available, it probably is best to assume that tassel-eared squirrels have a sex ratio approximating 50:50.

Age-ratio data were gathered on Abert squirrel populations on the Mogollon Rim each year from 1962 through 1981. Forelegs collected in hunter reporting boxes were mounted, X-rayed, and classified as adult or immature, based on the closure of the epiphyseal cartilage (Carson 1961).

With the exception of 1981, the percentage of immature squirrels in the harvest showed little annual variation. The percent young varied from 38% to 56% and averaged 45% (Table 2). If a 50:50 sex ratio is assumed, the young-to-female ratio would have ranged from 1.2 to 2.6 and averaged 1.6. Although these ratios are relatively constant compared to eastern squirrels, they do show enough variation in reproductive success to support the contention of Farentinos (1972a) and Stephenson (1975) that in some years not all adult females breed.

Table 2. Comparative Abert Squirrel Hunt Information from Hunt Data Collection Boxes, 1969–81

Information		East of Flagstaff											
	1969	1970	1971	1972[1]	1973	1974	1975[1]	1976	1977	1978	1979	1980	1981
No. of squirrel hunters reporting	166	204	187	81	94	57	101	249	380	406	182	88	186
Hunter days reported	212	276	256	136	149	89	162	376	520	541	262	124	240
Abert squirrels bagged	175	268	200	122	89	64	116	363	613	762	262	125	384
Abert squirrels per hunter	1.1	1.3	1.1	1.5	0.9	1.1	1.2	1.5	1.6	1.9	1.4	1.4	2.1
Abert squirrels per hunter per day	0.8	1.0	0.8	0.9	0.6	0.7	0.7	1.0	1.2	1.4	1.0	1.0	1.7
% immature Abert squirrels in harvest	44	38	45	45	45	54	42	56	46	37	38	42	21
No. of days of snow cover of 4 inches or more during previous winter[2]		15	23	14	85	33	39	36	19	22	49	39	19

[1]Squirrel foot and hunt data collection boxes were relocated in 1972 and 1975; quantitative data not comparable.

[2]The means of the Flagstaff and Heber climatological stations.

In 1981, only 21% (0.5 young: female) of the Abert squirrel population on the Mogollon Rim was young of the year. It would be interesting to know what factors triggered this poor reproductive performance. Especially intriguing is that the years of low recruitment (< 45% young) appear to have increased in recent years commensurate with an increase in the overall squirrel population as measured by hunt success (Table 2). Furthermore, there was no measurable relationship between reproductive success and subsequent population levels—the latter being determined largely by the mortality rate experienced during the previous winter.

Densities and home range. High-quality uncut forests can support tassel-eared squirrel densities of more than 100 squirrels per square mile, or one squirrel per six acres (Lawson 1941, Farentinos 1972a). Indeed, local densities of over one squirrel per two acres have been reported (Keith 1965)! More typically, one can expect densities in the neighborhood of between 15 and 30 squirrels per square mile, population levels depending as much on the severity of previous winters as on the carrying capacity of the habitat.

The size of the area used by each squirrel (= home range) depends on population density, suitability of the habitat, and food supply. Consequently, home ranges vary from season to season and year to year. Generally a squirrel's home range overlaps those of other squirrels and will be larger in winter than in summer (Farentinos 1979).

It is of interest that regardless of squirrel population levels at any given time, Trowbridge and Lawson (1942), Keith (1965), and Pederson et al. (1976) all found population densities to be from three to five times greater in virgin timber than in adjacent logged areas. An example of squirrel densities on the Mogollon Rim under pristine conditions was reported by F. P. Secrist in an 1896 article in *American Field:*

> *That evening was devoted to squirrel shooting, and there I found the place for the 38. Gray [Abert] squirrels were very plentiful. We [four men] killed thirty-six within a half mile of our camp. . . . Entering Winslow our load consisted of ten deer, twenty-nine turkeys, seventy-four ducks, about two hundred gray squirrels, and fifty rabbits.*

There is much overlap between home ranges and "territories" are not vigorously defended. Keith (1965), Patton (1975), Pederson et al. (1976), and Farentinos (1972a) found home ranges in good tassel-eared squirrel habitat to average between 6 and 24 acres. These investigators all found a greater average "home range" for males than for females. This was the case even outside the breeding season, and several females were found to have summer home ranges of less than five acres. During the mating season males wander outside of their normal home range, tripling the territory normally visited (Farentinos 1972b). Juveniles also wander in an attempt to locate and establish themselves in a territory.

Tassel-eared squirrel populations fluctuate annually and during the year. Squirrel density as measured by hunt success for the years 1969 through 1981 on the Mogollon Rim ranged from 0.9 to 2.1 squirrels per hunter trip (Table 2). During any given year the density of squirrels will be greatest in fall with the recruitment of young animals into the population, and least in spring after overwinter mortality.

Mortality. Predation, food failures, timber harvest, and sylvatic plague have all been suggested as being important mortality factors for tassel-eared squirrels. Although goshawks (*Accipiter gentilis*) and other predators have been documented as taking tassel-eared squirrels (Reynolds 1963), the actual instances of predation appear to be relatively few. There are no martens (*Martes americana*) or other specialized squirrel predators within the range of this squirrel—a fortunate circumstance, given the squirrel's lack of agility and the sparse cover of the habitat. Squirrels are occasionally found dead in the forest, but the most observable direct mortality is from road-kills, and paved highways through the pine forest take a heavy toll.

The greatest mortality factor however, is snow cover. Severe declines in tassel-eared squirrel numbers were reported for the winters of 1918–19 by Rasmussen (1941:257) and 1953–54 by Keith (1965). The latter noted that squirrels captured the following spring exhibited shocklike systems and several died when stressed for more than a few minutes. Similar losses occurred when trapping Kaibab squirrels during the severe winter of 1972–73. Stephenson (1975) suggested that winter mortality of

Abert squirrels might be related to the amount and duration of snow cover, as deep snow could affect feeding habits and limit the availability of quality foods.

Stephenson and Brown (1980) later found annual mortality to vary from 22 to 66% of the population, and that these changes were significantly correlated to the number of days of snow cover of four inches or more. This one factor explained more than 70% of the variation in annual mortality!

Because no relationship was found between variations in recruitment and changes in population levels, we reasoned that squirrel numbers in any given year were largely dependent on base population levels the previous fall and snow-induced mortality the following winter. Although snow cover is not directly responsible for mortality, it forces the squirrels to rely for extended periods on inner bark. With a steady diet of only this source, the squirrels lose weight, eventually become stressed, and succumb at an increased rate.

Census Techniques

A means of indexing population levels other than measuring hunt success is to census twig clippings (Brown 1982b). Plots on the Kaibab Plateau and an area north of Happy Jack on the Coconino National Forest were cleared of squirrel clippings in September, and twig clipping counts were made the following June after snowmelt.

A clipping-count index during the 8 years of surveys on the Kaibab Plateau varied, as did days snow cover (Table 3). These data indicated a marked decline in squirrel clipping activity in spring 1973 and a relatively low level thereafter. This decline was preceded by heavy snows during the winter of 1972–73. The relatively large number of clippings recorded in 1972 was preceded by a winter of light snowfall. Although 1971–72 snow cover data were not available from the North Kaibab Plateau, data from Grand Canyon National Park (South Rim) indicated snow cover of <100 days for that winter and for the two years previous. Relatively heavy snow cover occurred on the Kaibab during all winters of the study after 1972–73.

Comparison of the clipping-count index with squirrels seen

Table 3. Clipping-count and Snow Cover Data, Kaibab Plateau, Arizona

	1972	1973	1974	1975	1976	1977	1978	1979
Clipping-count index	410	42	22	11	23	18	12	13
Mean N days snow cover ≥ 1 inch previous winter	53	192[a]	137	196	153	101	156[a]	188
Squirrels seen during clipping count	ND[b]	17	7	7	12	8	15	ND[b]

[a] Estimated
[b] No data.

on the survey was not significantly related ($r = 0.57$, $p \leqslant 0.10$). No other population level measurements were available for the North Kaibab.

Clipping-count, snow cover, and hunting success data from Happy Jack also varied (Table 4). As on the Kaibab, a decline in squirrel clippings was recorded in 1973 concomitant with heavy snow cover the previous winter. This decline was followed by a reduction in hunting success the following autumn; squirrel population levels in this area were subject to an estimated mortality rate of 66% between autumn 1972 and autumn 1973 (Stephenson and Brown 1980). There was a significant correlation ($r = 0.97$ $p < 0.05$) between the clipping-count index and hunting success over the 4-year period. This relationship indicates that the clipping-count index could be a reliable survey technique if it is assumed that hunting success represents squirrel density.

Since this species has limited and relatively consistent recruitment rates, the clipping-count index in any given year is largely dependent on the number of squirrels present the previous year; i.e., a large number of clippings cannot be present

Table 4. Clipping-count, Snow Cover, and Hunter Success Data, Happy Jack, Arizona

	1972	1973	1974	1975
Clipping-count index	260	12	40	112
N days snow cover ≥ 4 inches previous winter	14	85	33	39
Squirrels per hunter trip subsequent autumn	1.51	0.95	1.12	1.15

without a sizable number of adult squirrels available. Conversely, a low population of squirrels produces fewer clippings even if their diet of inner bark increases.

Pederson et al. (1976:27) and others have suggested that the number of clippings may be more a function of scarcity of other food items than a measure of squirrel numbers. Because squirrels feed exclusively on inner bark during periods of extended snow cover, the number of clippings per squirrel probably does increase during winters of heavy snow. Clipping-count indices, however, decreased or remained at low levels after such winters—dramatically so after winters of extremely heavy snow cover. Apparently the clipping-count index also reflects overwinter mortality and is a reliable indicator of reduced spring population numbers.

Clipping counts on randomly located transects provide at least gross indices of tassel-eared squirrel population trends. The technique is time-consuming and costly, but appears to be the best available method to measure population changes in unhunted areas. The arbitrary use of days of snow cover to calculate the index does not consider years when snow cover is nearly or completely lacking. This survey technique may not be appropriate under these conditions. Also, the potential for squirrel movement and variation in diet means that clipping count indices may not measure local and/or moderate changes in population levels.

Effects on Forest Silviculture

Because of the squirrel's feeding habits, some foresters have complained that tassel-eared squirrels damage commercially valuable trees and interfere with good forestry practices (see, e.g., Bailey 1931, Coughlin 1938, Pearson 1950). Most concerns have centered on the weakening and even death of excessively clipped feed trees (Trowbridge and Lawson 1942), and the depletion of pine seed through cone cutting (Larson and Schubert 1970). J. Stokely Ligon (1927), even proposed squirrel control measures because squirrel clippings were ingested by cows and the needles caused the abortion of calves!

34

Larson and Schubert (1970) thought Abert squirrels extremely destructive to cone crops because they "destroyed" more than 20% of 10 years of cone production. They found that in one year as much as 75% of the annual cone crop was cut, and that cone feeding trees were those with the most cones. Also, squirrels selected the largest and best cones. They considered twig-clipping less destructive, although conelets discarded with the terminal clippings meant a decrease in the following year's cone crop.

Although damage to individual trees may be impressive (Fig. 14), few trees are actually killed by squirrels. Larson and Schubert (1970) and Hall (1981) each noted only one tree killed in this manner during their separate 10-year investigations. Their principal concern for twig-clipped trees was the heavy crown damage. Pearson (1950) reported that from 37% to 47% of the trees on two experimental plots were severely damaged by squirrels. Such trees would be stressed, grow at reduced rates and might be less likely to survive infestations of pandora moths (*Coloradia pandora*), bark beetles (*Dendroctonus* spp.), and other pests.

Goldman (1928), Pearson (1950), and Keith (1965) all noted that squirrels showed a preference to feed on certain trees. Larson and Schubert (1970) and later Hall (1981) determined that although almost all trees were "tasted," the preference for particular trees was not only seasonal but most often extended from one year to the next. These findings contrasted with those of Ffolliott and Patton (1978), who found a "rotation of use" among feed trees. Farentinos et al. (1981) reported that the twigs from these "feed trees" contained significantly less monoterpenes— mildly toxic secondary organic compounds—than nonselected trees. Hall (1981) also found striking variations in monoterpenes between individual trees but was unable to relate differences between feed trees and other trees to any individual monoterpene. Hall though that the larger ratio of sugars to nonsugar substances in the phloem of feed trees coupled with the inhibiting effects of bitter monoterpenes might play a dual role in tree selection.

Hall (1981) found that trees that were fed on did have less vigor and lower growth rates than comparable trees that were not. These stresses were alleviated, however, by gradual changes

Figure 14. Ponderosa pine subjected to heavy clipping use by a tassel-eared squirrel. The tree has been more than 70% defoliated.

in squirrel feeding patterns and periodic decreases in squirrel population levels so that the trees recovered over time. Hall characterized the overall effect of squirrel feeding as causing detectable but insignificant tree damage when compared to other factors. He found no significant differences in either the trees or the forest on Shiva Temple, an isolated pine forest devoid of squirrels, than on comparable, inhabited sites. Perhaps more importantly, he questioned how an animal that coevolved with such a specific habitat could jeopardize that habitat. Like Bailey (1931) 50 years earlier, Hall suggested that the squirrels likely were of more benefit than detriment to ponderosa pine regeneration and had a symbiotic relationship with the forest.

Actually, it is the forester whose tree management threatens the squirrel. Conservative logging, including even such long-accepted practices as selective cutting on a 120-year rotation may be detrimental to a squirrel and tree that coevolved as climax species. The intensive forestry practices being implemented in the 1980s will almost certainly have a negative impact. Especially at lower elevations and in the more xeric sites, squirrel numbers and distribution will suffer with the elimination of old growth ponderosa pines and poor or sporadic regeneration of new forests.

Figure 15. Portrait of an adult Chiricahua fox squirrel. (Photo by Guy Bailey.)

The Fox Squirrels

Sciurus arizonensis and *Sciurus apache*

ARIZONA'S FOX SQUIRRELS—the Arizona gray and Chiricahua fox squirrel—are allopatric (= geographically separated) color variants of what are the same, or two very similar species. Animals south and east of the Yaqui River drainage, including the Chiricahua Mountains, are a grizzled yellow to russet orange (Fig. 15). This is especially so on the underparts, and the animal "looks like a fox squirrel." To the north and west, the squirrels are a grizzled silvery gray with white underparts and are known as Arizona grays because of their "gray squirrel" appearance and state of primary residence (Fig. 16). In essence, these squirrels duplicate the Kaibab squirrel phenomenon—differently colored individuals of a variable species became isolated or invaded "new" habitat; their similarly colored progeny continued to occupy that habitat and whatever new range became successively available.

The history of the discovery and nomenclature of these squirrels is of interest. The type specimen of the Arizona gray squirrel was collected at the head of Hassayampa Creek by Willard Rice for Elliot Coues in 1865 (Davis 1982). Coues (1867) considered the squirrel "quite rare" and, except for another specimen obtained by Rice and two taken by Ferdinand Bischoff in 1871, no other animals were collected until the mid-1880s. Most of these were collected by, or for, E. A. Mearns in the Weber and Fossil Creek areas under the Mogollon Rim. Both Mearns (1907) and E. W. Nelson, who collected a specimen at the headwaters of the San Francisco River in New Mexico, considered the squirrel to be "rare."

In the 1890s the *huachuca* race of this squirrel was collected and described as occurring only in the Huachuca Mountains (Allen 1894, Mearns 1907). A great collector, Herbert Brown, obtained a specimen on the east side of the Catalina Mountains for E. W. Nelson, but this slightly smaller race (*S. a. catalinae*) wasn't described for the Catalina, Rincon, and Santa Rita mountains until many years later (Doutt 1931). In the meantime, "Huachuca grays" had been discovered in the Pajarito, Patagonia, and Canelo mountains in southern Arizona and in the mountains of northern Sonora.

Also in the 1890s, a new species of fox squirrel was described for northern Mexico. This animal was taken on the Lumholtz expedition to northern Sonora and Chihuahua by a Mr. Robinette and described by Allen (1893) as *Sciurus apache*. Mearns also collected a series of *S. apache* in 1892 and 1893 in the San Luis Mountains in Chihuahua near Monument #65 on the U.S.-Mexico border. Shortly afterward, A. K. Fisher collected a specimen of the squirrel from the Chiricahua Mountains, Arizona. This latter population was later described as a separate species (*Sciurus chiricahuae* by Goldman (1933a, 1933b) on the basis of isolation, a shorter and broader rostrum, and more richly colored underparts. Nonetheless, there is no single character of *S. chiricahuae* that cannot be duplicated in a specimen of *S. apache* (Lee and Hoffmeister 1963).

Arizona gray squirrel populations in the Patagonia, Huachuca, and other mountains in southern Arizona and in Sonora are still considered a separate subspecies, *huachuca* (Allen 1895); those in the Catalina, Rincon, and Santa Rita mountains are designated as subspecies *catalinae* (Doutt 1931). Although *catalinae* specimens are measurably smaller, it is doubtful if *huachuca* is measurably different from *S. a. arizonensis* populations in central Arizona and Catron County, New Mexico (Hoffmeister 1984). Our examination of ca. 200

specimens from throughout the species' range showed little predictable variation in pelage or measurements among any of these subspecies. As for reproductive isolation, several populations, both within and between the described subspecies, are allopatric and have been so for some time.

Sciurus apache and S. chiricahuae were combined by Lee and Hoffmeister (1963) with an earlier described species, taken in Zacatecas, Mexico, but named S. nayaritensis. They noted considerable variation in color between, and among, apache and nayaritensis (including white-bellied gray morphs of nayaritensis), and relegated chiricahuae and apache to subspecific status of nayaritensis. These mammalogists stated tht these squirrels were obviously closely related to the eastern fox squirrel (Sciurus niger) and the two species might be conspecific. If so, the Arizona gray might also be included as S. niger arizonensis. This would avoid the incongruity of sub-Mogollon and Madrean squirrels having the species name of nayaritensis and being represented by an uncharacteristic type specimen collected at the extreme southern limits of the species' range.

Until further study, the arizonensis taxon is recommended to be retained for the white-bellied gray morphs of Arizona, New Mexico, and Sonora. The apache designation should be used for Madrean squirrels north of the Rio Mesquital in Durango, Mexico, including the isolated chiricahuae subspecies (Fig. 17). Otherwise, both species should be considered subspecies of S. niger.

Descriptions

The Arizona gray squirrel is a large, white-bellied squirrel with a noticeably full, bushy tail. It has a white eye-ring and superficially resembles an Abert squirrel, with shorter, rounded ears. Indeed, the pelage of the two is strikingly similar, considering the different habitats occupied and their long evolutionary separation. Unlike the Abert squirrel, there is no black lateral line on the flanks separating the body's dorsal pelage from the white underparts. The feet are also more flecked with gray, and this criterion along can be used to differentiate the species. The upper parts, especially in winter, are a beautiful salt-and-

41

Figure 16. Portrait of a young Arizona gray squirrel. (Photo by Harry Biller.)

peppered steel gray, in contrast to the more charcoal gray of the Abert squirrel; the handsome tail is fringed in white. These white outer hairs are separated from the gray basal hairs by a distinct black border.

A fox squirrel heritage is evidenced by the general shape and appearance of the head, and by the underside of the tail, the inner hairs of which, in all seasons, are a russet orange-brown. Some ochre or russet brown is also usually present between the ears, elsewhere on the head, and, most noticeably, on the back. Unlike other fox squirrels, including those in Mexico, no black or other strikingly different color morphs are known for Arizona grays. Pelage coloration does, however, vary by season, location, and individual (Fig. 18). Generally, *huachuca* specimens have little or no rufous brown below the shoulders and present more of a silver gray back than their more northern relatives. Rarely is there also any rufous on the hind quarters of *huachuca*, as in *arizonensis* or *catalinae*, and the overall appearance is of a "grayer" squirrel. There are, nonetheless, animals in both populations that would be difficult to differentiate to subspecies, particularly in summer.

As with other sciurids, there are two molts a year. The more luxuriant winter pelage is present from about November through mid-April. In summer the fur is less grizzled, the animal appears more brownish, and the tail is less plumelike.

The Chiricahua fox squirrel is almost identical in appearance except that the Arizona gray's white parts are colored a russet to cinnamon orange. The grizzled marks are as in the gray "Arizona" phase, and all markings are essentially the same in both forms.

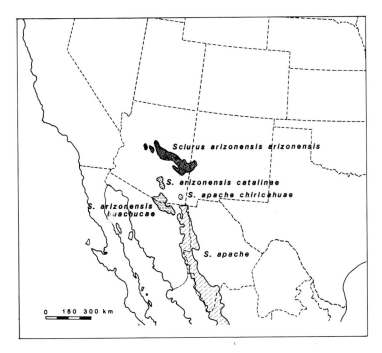

Figure 17. Distribution of *Sciurus arizonensis* and *Sciurus apache*.

43

A sample of more than 100 adult Arizona gray squirrels averaged 23.1 ounces (22.3 ounces excluding stomachs and stomach contents). The lightest adult weighed 18.6 ounces, the heaviest, an adult male, 31.2 ounces. A smaller sample of Chiricahua fox squirrels averaged slightly more—24.9 ounces, but the range was within that of the collected grays. Adult gray squirrels averaged 20 inches in total length; Chiricahua fox squirrels averaged about 21 inches. About 50% of the length of both squirrels is made up by the tail.

Behavior. Both Arizona gray squirrels and Chiricahua fox squirrels can be secretive or readily observed, depending on their feeding habits and time of year. Like Arizona's other squirrels, they can be especially difficult to locate during early summer, when the females are pregnant and nursing young. The squirrels can also be shy and hard to find in winter, when their forest homes are bare and open to scrutiny. At other times, when feeding on alder (*Alnus oblongifolia*) buds at the ends of branches, when foraging for acorns or walnuts, when engaged in mating chases, or when artificially fed, the squirrels can be conspicuous.

When danger approaches, the squirrel's normal defense response is to remain motionless. This tendency to "freeze" even when in clear view has led some to consider the Chiricahua squirrel unhabituated to humans and in need of special protection (e.g., Cahalane 1939). Actually, this "fool quail" like response is found in both squirrels and is an effective defense; many more squirrels are passed by than observed. This is especially so when the animals are feeding high in the trees 60 feet or more above the ground.

When caught out in the open or fired at, the squirrels make for the tallest trees and disappear behind a large bough or in a den cavity. Frightened animals will remain hidden and motionless for 45 minutes or more. I once watched two individuals remain lying flat on a branch for 1 hour and 15 minutes. At the end of that time one animal still had not moved and gave no indication of being ready to reveal himself.

Silence, too, is the rule, and except for the chucking and barking alarm calls of a nervous squirrel, the animals are comparatively silent. Vocalization defeats the purpose of camouflage and a motionless defense. When the squirrels are vocal, they are invariably in a tree and responding to some man or animal intruder. Alarm barks vary among individuals but generally are more "raspy" and gruff than the "quirk" calls of the Abert squirrel and may be followed by a "whirring" screech or scream. Hobbs (1980) studied alarm calling behavior and concluded that these squirrels were more likely to call when sound carried well and the calling squirrel was concealed or felt secure. She found the squirrels to be more vocal in summer than in winter and attributed this behavior to habitat characteristics and kin selection; young squirrels would be those most likely to benefit from a parent's calling behavior.

Food habits. Arizona grays and Chiricahua fox squirrels are foragers; they do not cache food, nor do they regularly bury nuts like their eastern cousins. Indeed, there is little reason for them to do so, as their habitat is relatively snow-free. Barry Spicer (pers. comm.) nonetheless did observe Arizona gray squirrels burying individual acorns in leaf litter on three occasions. Mast (walnuts, acorns, juniper berries, hackberries, and pine seeds) is taken throughout the year and comprises 67% of the squirrels' total diet (Fig. 19). Fungi, both subterranean and emergent species, are also important year-long foods and were found in 51 of 182 collected stomachs (Table 5).

Flower parts were seasonally important and coincided with the breeding season (Table 5). It is suspected that these contain vitamin A and other vitamins that stimulate reproductive activity after a period of quiescence. This would be consistent with the findings for other species (e.g., Gambel quail, Hungerford 1964) and analogous to the tassel-eared squirrel feeding on the staminate flowers of ponderosa pine and the red squirrel feeding on spruce flowers just prior to and during their period of sexual activity.

Riparian trees and associated plants in sub-Mogollon Arizona have a prolonged flowering season, beginning with manzanita and alder in late winter and early spring, and progressing through maples, sycamores, ashes, and walnuts (Fig. 20). In February and March, squirrels can often be spotted as they crouch exposed at the ends of alder branches feeding on the new buds and staminate flowers. By April and May, blooming is well

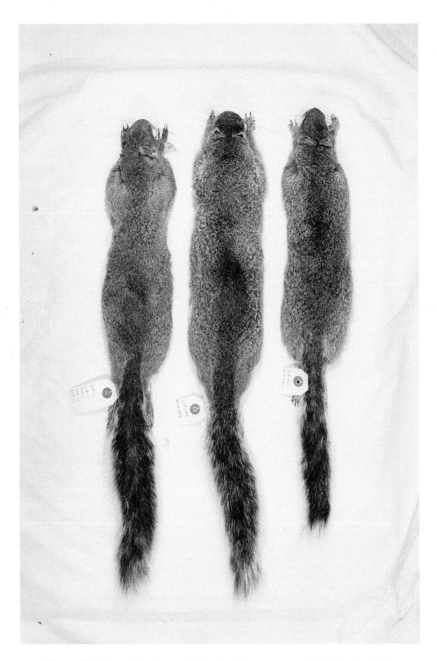

Figure 18. Size and pelage variation in Arizona gray squirrels. *Left to right:* adult male from the Bradshaw Mountains, October; adult male from the Huachuca Mountains, February; immature female from Beaver Creek, November.

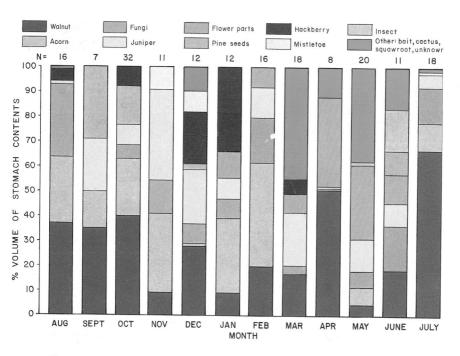

Figure 19. Foods found in the stomachs of Arizona fox squirrels, by month.

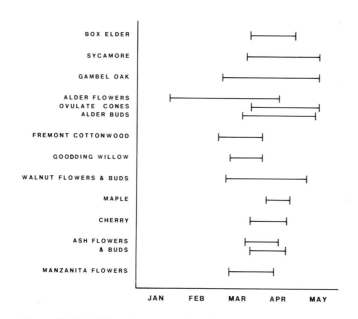

Figure 20. Typical flowering progression of some riparian deciduous trees.

Table 5. Monthly Stomach Contents of Arizona Gray Squirrels, 1979–82

Material		Jan.	Feb.	Mar.	Apr.	May	June	July	Aug.	Sep.	Oct.	Nov.	Dec.	Mean/Total
Walnut	% vol	8.4	21.2	16.9	50.6	4.6	18.2	66.8	37.5	35.7	41.4	8.3	27.9	28.1
	Freq	4	4	5	5	4	2	15	7	3	15	2	5	71
Acorn	% vol	32.7	41.2	—	—	6.4	—	11.1	26.6	14.3	20.8	29.2	0.4	15.2
	Freq	6	6	—	—	3	—	2	5	1	7	4	1	35
Juniper berries	% vol	7.2	11.2	18.4	0.4	12.4	9.5	5.6	0.4	21.4	8.6	41.7	19.8	13.0
	Freq	2	3	7	1	5	3	1	2	2	5	5	4	40
Fungi	% vol	8.4	18.8	3.2	0.3	8.8	18.0	14.2	29.3	—	5.4	12.5	8.6	10.6
	Freq	5	6	3	1	6	4	8	6	—	6	3	3	51
Flower buds	% vol	10.0	7.6	7.8	36.9	30.7	11.8	—	—	—	—	—	—	9.0
	Freq	2	1	2	3	9	2	—	—	—	—	—	—	19
Hackberry	% vol	33.3	—	5.6	—	—	—	—	5.6	—	7.7	—	18.5	5.9
	Freq	5	—	1	—	—	—	—	1	—	3	—	4	14
Pine seeds	% vol	—	—	—	—	—	9.1	t	—	28.6	15.8	—	2.5	4.7
	Freq	—	—	—	—	—	1	—	—	2	6	—	1	10
Mistletoe	% vol	—	—	—	—	—	—	0.6	—	—	—	8.3	8.2	1.4
	Freq	—	—	—	—	—	—	1	—	—	—	1	1	3
Unknown	% vol	—	—	2.8	—	—	—	t	0.6	—	0.3	—	5.8	0.8
	Freq	—	—	1	—	—	—	—	1	—	1	—	1	4
Squaw root	% vol	—	—	—	—	—	—	1.7	—	—	—	—	t	0.1
	Freq	—	—	—	—	—	—	1	—	—	—	—	—	1
Insect	% vol	—	—	—	—	0.2	16.8	—	—	—	—	—	—	1.4
	Freq	—	—	—	—	1	4	—	—	—	—	—	—	5
Cactus	% vol	—	—	—	—	—	0.2	—	—	—	—	—	—	0.2
	Freq	—	—	—	—	—	1	—	—	—	—	—	—	1
Bait	% vol	—	—	42.5	11.9	36.9	16.4	—	—	—	—	—	8.4	9.7
	Freq	—	—	10	1	8	2	—	—	—	—	—	2	23
Stomachs observed (total)		15	13	18	8	21	11	18	16	7	31	12	12	182

advanced among several deciduous trees, and the newly emerging leaves provide cover during the breeding season. Later, during the summer months, insects and other animal matter supplement a mast diet.

Pine seeds begin showing up in the diet in June, and these items are eaten through the fall and even into the winter months (Fig. 21). Seeds may be gleaned from cones of ponderosa pine, Apache pine *(Pinus latifolia)*, and Mexican white pine, as well as from white-fir and perhaps other conifers. In late fall (November-December), juniper berries, hackberries, mistletoe, and fungi are taken. Walnuts and acorns are the mainstay of Arizona gray squirrels, however, and as Mearns (1907) observed, "walnuts, a preferred food, stain the pelage."

Figure 21. Ponderosa pine cone feeding detritus of the Apache fox squirrel. The shucked ponderosa pine cones are similar to those left by Abert squirrels. Although Arizona fox squirrels occasionally feed on inner-bark, dropping terminal needle clusters to the ground, they rarely, if ever, leave the "peeled" segments of twigs so characteristic of Abert squirrels.

Nests. Each squirrel may have several leaf nests or none, depending on the availability of den trees. Two types of nests are constructed: a flat platform-type structure used for resting in summer, and a more substantial, covered, bolus nest. The latter type nest appears to be in lieu of a suitable den site and is used as a nursery in addition to a "home." These nests can be differentiated from hawk nets by their location in the tree and dome shape.

Nests were observed in sycamores, walnut trees, alders, maples, cottonwoods, ash trees, and Apache pines, but most commonly in various species of oak. Nest trees were all more than 40 feet tall, and the nests from 30 to 100 feet above the ground—mostly between 35 and 60 feet. Typical locations were at the fork of two or more substantial branches, or in the crotch formed by the trunk and a major branch. At least in central Arizona, there appears to be a tendency to favor the south or southwest side of the tree.

Construction is accomplished by the squirrel carrying small branches in its mouth to the nest site. These are inserted into the fork and woven into smaller branches and other twigs until a crude platform is created. Leaves (usually those of the tree in which the nest is located) and more twigs are added until the nest is about 12 inches in diameter and up to 2 feet in height (Fig. 22). Shredded bark, string, grass, and spider webs may interlace and line the more substantial nests. An entrance hole of from 2 to 4 inches, just enough to admit the squirrel, allows access to a chamber formed by the squirrel's body.

Distribution

The Arizona gray is appropriately named. Except for north central Sonora and the watersheds of the San Francisco and Gila River drainages in Catron and Pinos Altos counties, New Mexico, this squirrel is confined to our state (Fig. 23). Here its major distribution is along pine-headed drainages below the Mogollon Rim, with disjunct populations in some of the larger mountain ranges in southern Arizona and northern Sonora. In Arizona, these include the Catalina, Rincon, Santa Rita, Patagonia, Huachuca, and Bradshaw mountains, and Pine

Figure 22. Typical nest of an Arizona fox squirrel. The tree limb, leaves, and twig material are oak; string and shredded juniper bark were used to line the nest.

Mountain on the Prescott National Forest. Interestingly, these squirrels are absent from the Pinaleño (= Graham), Galiuro, Pinal, and a number of other mountain ranges possessing pines, oaks, and riparian habitats that appear suitable for them (e.g., Mingus Mountain and Aravaipa and Redfield canyons). There is little evidence that Arizona grays have increased their distribution in recent times as has the sympatric Abert squirrel. Although a number of new locales and range extensions were documented (Fig. 23), these may be due only to the paucity of earlier collections. We were, however, unable to find Arizona grays at Yank Springs in Sycamore Canyon west of the Pajarito Mountains, where an immature male was collected by VanRossem in 1945 (Cockrum 1960) and where Goodpaster shot three out of a nest in 1961 (Hoffmeister 1984).

The distribution of Arizona grays in Sonora is imperfectly known; museum specimens have been colleced from the Sierra de los Ajos, Sierra Azul, Sierra de la Madera, Sierra Patagonia, and Sierra de Piñitos (Caire 1978). There are reliable observations as far south as the mountains northeast of Cucúrpe (T. R. Van Devender, pers. comm.).

In the Chiricahua Mountains and in the mountains and

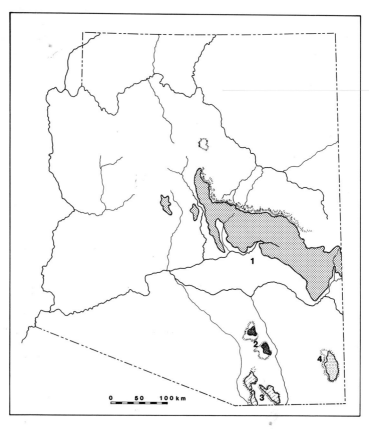

Figure 23. Distribution of the Arizona fox squirrels. **1.** *Sciurus arizonensis arizonensis;* **2.** *S. a. catalinae;* **3.** *S. a. huachuca;* **4.** *S. apache chiricahuae.*

canyons of extreme northeast Sonora (e.g., the Sierra Tigre, Sierra San Luis, and Cajon Bonita), and in the Sierra Madre Occidental, the Arizona gray squirrel is replaced by the closely related Apache fox squirrel.

Habitat. Both the Arizona gray squirrel and Chiricahua fox squirrel are associated with the denser mixed broadleaf communities of riparian deciduous forest (Figs. 24, 25). Even within deciduous forest the squirrels are generally restricted to the upper elevations between 5,000 and 6,500 feet, where the hardwoods are in juxtaposition with montane forest or evergreen woodlands that approach or achieve the physiognomy of forest (Fig. 26). Sizable populations extend downward along stream-

52

Figure 24. Riparian habitat of the Arizona gray squirrel—Sycamore Creek west of Pine Mountain, summer aspect.

sides into semidesert grassland and chaparral only where the riparian forest exhibits species diversity and tall, interlocking canopies. The squirrels are lacking in the more open, flood-prone woodlands and in the less diverse cottonwood-willow communities downstream. Accordingly, the altitudinal limits for Arizona fox squirrels are the limits of mixed broadleaf and adjacent montane communities—3,500 to 7,500 feet—somewhat higher in southern Arizona to ca. 8,500 feet.

Figure 25. Riparian habitat of the Arizona gray squirrel along Beaver Creek in Yavapai County—winter aspect.

As befits an arboreal species, the squirrels prefer mature forests of tall (to over 75 feet) and decadent trees. Primary residence is therefore on the older alluvial benches of well-watered drainages, at adjacent springs and seeps, and in well-wooded uplands. Favored habitats are groves of old cavity-prone Arizona sycamores *(Platanus wrightii)* and other large broadleaf deciduous trees—narrowleaf and Fremont cottonwood *(Populus angustifolia, P. fremonti)*, box elder *(Acer negundo)*, Arizona alder, big-tooth maple *(Acer grandidentatum)*, ash *(Faxinus velutina)*, willows *(Salix* spp.), and Arizona walnut *(Juglans major)*. Two arboreal dominants of the higher montane forest—

Figure 26. Forest aspect of the Arizona gray squirrel—P.B. Creek in the Sierra Ancha, fall 1980. Photo by R. Rice.

ponderosa pine and Gambel oak—frequently extend downward to participate in the riparian forest community and in these situations these two trees are used extensively by the squirrels.

Trees of somewhat less stature, including alligator-bark juniper *(Juniperus deppeana)*, pinyon pine *(Pinus edulis, P. cembroides)*, Arizona cypress *(Cupressus arizonica)*, cherry *(Prunus* spp.), and hackberry *(Celtis reticulata)*, seasonally provide mast and/or facilitate arboreal movement. Wild grape *(Vitus arizonica)*, Virginia creeper *(Parthenocissus inserta)*, and other vines may festoon the trees; scarlet sumac *(Rhus glabra)* often provides a low midstory aspect. The overall impression is that of a woodlot in the eastern deciduous forest. Depending on the amount and intensity of livestock grazing, the understory may be herbaceous and luxuriant or present a barren, "eaten-out" appearance.

55

The presence of large evergreen oaks (*Quercus arizonica*, *Q. emoryi*, *Q. grisea*), while not always conspicuous, appears universal throughout the range of the squirrels and is perhaps essential. Although the Arizona walnut has been considered a key indicator of gray squirrel distribution, an equal case can be made for Arizona oak. These large hardwoods (to 80 feet), along with the deciduous Gambel oak, provide crucial sources of mast, cavities, and nest platforms. Southward, with the greater development of tall Madrean oaks on the uplands, and the addition of madroño (*Arbutus arizonica*), silverleaf oak (*Q. hypoleucoides*), and netleaf oak (*Q. rugosa*), both fox squirrels may exist away from deciduous trees (Fig. 27). Similarly, in the north, Arizona gray squirrels may be found in groves of large Gambel oaks with riparian species essentially absent.

Figure 27. Oak woodland inhabited by the Chiricahua fox squirrel. *Tall* oaks of *Quercus arizonica, Q. hypoleuca, Q. rugosa,* and *Q. emoryi* provide mast, nest sites, and escape cover for *Sciurus apache chiricahuae* and *Sciurus arizonensis huachuca.*

Figure 28. Staminate flowers of Arizona alder—early March 1981. Emerging flowers and buds of this winter deciduous tree are a mainstay for the Arizona gray squirrel in late winter and early spring and are associated with breeding activity.

From the Catalina Mountains north, the distribution of Arizona grays is also often associated with Arizona alder. This tree, along with oaks and walnut, appears to be important, as squirrel records are lacking from alderless areas. There are, however, areas of alders where there are no squirrels and, again, diversity and the inclusion of pines and oaks appears to be an essential ingredient of gray squirrel habitat. Perhaps the monoecious alder, with its early buds and late winter flowers, provides an important winter-spring food source at the squirrel's northern and western range (Fig. 28). Southward in the Santa

Rita, Rincon, and Huachuca mountains and in other southern Arizona locales, big-tooth maples, a greater diversity of large mast-producing oaks, and the late-fruiting madroño, may compensate for the lack of alders.

Life History

Until recently, little was known of the life history of these squirrels. This scarcity of data has been rectified somewhat by a two-year study of Arizona gray squirrel reproduction and food habits (Theobald 1983). Much remains to be learned, but some discussion of the animal's feeding, reproductive behavior, and habitat requirements is now possible. Work is still needed on the animal's social behavior, population dynamics, and limiting factors.

Recruitment. Unlike eastern fox and gray squirrels, there is no evidence of fall litters in Arizona fox squirrels (see, e.g., Madson 1964). Examination of reproductive organs showed the period of sexual activity to be from January through June (Fig. 29). Although subadult females appear to breed later in their second year than adults, no evidence was found of any female having more than one litter per year. The absence of placental scars in some summer-collected adults indicated that not all females breed each year; mature sperm was present from November through July, peaking in April.

The onset of breeding activity was correlated with flower emergence and flower parts in the diet (Fig. 29). Although an increase in cervix width and bulbourethral gland weights indicated breeding capability as early as January and February (with the flowering of manzanita (*Arctostaphlos pungens?*), estrus for most collected squirrels was in April and early May. This was also the time that mating chases have been observed: April 8, 1943, at Summerhaven in the Catalina Mountains (Arrington 1943); February 7, April 25, and May 13, 1976, in the Catalina Mountains (Barry Spicer, pers. comm.); five males and one female on May 2, 1983, at O'Donnell Cienega.

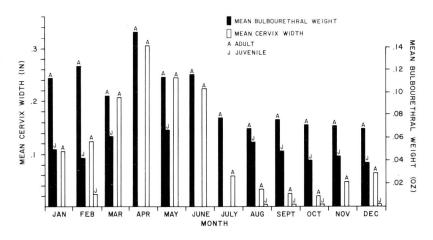

Figure 29. Breeding season of Arizona gray squirrels as determined from cervix width and bulbourethral weights.

Female Arizona gray squirrels with embryos were collected each month from January through June, with most pregnant females (58%) collected in May and June. Both Mearns (1907) and Caire (1978) collected pregnant Apache fox squirrels in July and cervix data indicated that some Arizona grays also would have been pregnant that month.

In our collection, of 15 pregnant females of both species, there were 46 embryos, or 3.1 fetuses per female (range 2–4). In comparison, 36 adult females had 118 placental scars, or 3.3 embryos per female, indicating some prenatal loss. During 1979 and 1980, lactating females were collected between June 27 and October 17. The earliest that a juvenile was observed and collected was on June 24, indicating a variable and prolonged natal period similar to that of the tassel-eared squirrel.

Population characteristics. Collections of 274 mostly shot specimens taken throughout the state yielded 134 males and 140 females, a sex ratio not significantly different from 1:1. Of 214 accurately aged squirrels, 40 were juveniles (19%), 26 were subadults (12%), and 148 were adults (69%). The percent young among 108 fall-winter (October–February) collected squirrels was 42.6%, or 1.5 young squirrels per adult female, assuming a sex ration of 1:1. This recruitment rate closely approximates that for tassel-eared squirrels.

Densities. Neither the Arizona gray nor the Apache fox squirrel has ever been reported to be a common species. Coues (1867) described the Arizona gray as one of the rarest animals in Arizona, and Cahalane (1939) held the same opinion for the Chiricahua fox squirrel. Because of their linear occurrence along drainageways, the density of Arizona's fox squirrels is difficult to determine. There have been no marking studies and no measurements of population numbers. Most investigators believe that populations fluctuate with available food supplies and vary from year to year (see, e.g., Monson 1972). Large densities of squirrels have been observed in Ramsey Canyon in the Huachuca Mountains, in summer home areas near Pine, and in other human supplied feeding areas. Densities may also be high in quality habitats; as many as six squirrels were taken in less than an hour from one stand of tall, mature trees at springs near Fossil Creek. Conversely, densities appear to be low in oak woodlands with widely separated riparian areas.

Only one report is known of a "squirrel migration" in Arizona as has been described for high-density eastern gray squirrel and occasionally eastern fox squirrel populations. Stewart Daniels reported in "influx" of gray squirrels near Fossil Creek during March and April 1886, during which "numbers of squirrels" were seen daily (Mearns 1907). There have been no such reports since.

Mortality. Both goshawks (Hobbs 1980) and red-tailed hawks (*Buteo jamaicensis*) (R. K. Barsch, pers. comm.) have been observed taking Arizona gray squirrels. I observed a bobcat (*Felis rufus*) carrying a freshly killed Arizona gray along Horton Creek in late September 1970. This was shortly after the "Labor Day flood," which destroyed much of the riparian community, possibly necessitating the squirrel foraging on the ground and increasing the opportunity for predation. Far more squirrels have been observed as road kills, and adult squirrels have few natural enemies proficient in their capture.

As with other tree squirrels, habitat quality and food supplies appear to be the principal limiting factors. It is suspected that most squirrels meet their fate by dispersing to unsuitable habitat in an attempt to locate or establish a home range. The mechanics of this pheonomenon are unknown and would make for interesting study.

Figure 30. Portraits of two red squirrels. **A.** Squirrel in winter pelage by Robert Vahle; **B.** Squirrel in summer pelage by Robert Hernbrode (note the molt pattern across the lower 1/3 of the animal).

The Red Squirrel

Tamiasciurus hudsonicus

WIDELY DISTRIBUTED IN NORTH AMERICA, this squirrel is commonly known in the Rocky Mountain states as chickaree, spruce squirrel, or pine squirrel (Fig. 30). These local names refer to the animal's chattering call and the fact that it is most often found in subalpine conifer forests of spruce and fir or in lodgepole and white pines. In the Northeast, where the species was first described, the animal's upper parts are red-orange, hence the common name.

The white-bellied red squirrel and its close relative, the yellow- or orange-bellied Douglas squirrel (*Tamiasciurus douglasi*), enjoy a large range in western North America (Fig. 31). This has resulted in a number of subspecies being recognized, two red squirrels of which occur in Arizona. The Arizona chickaree (*T. hudsonicus mogollonensis*) is found throughout northern Arizona and New Mexico. The "type" specimen was collected on May 25, 1887, by E. A. Mearns at Quaking Aspen settlement at the summit of the "Mogollon Mountains" (= Rim) in central Arizona. The other subspecies, the Graham Mountain spruce squirrel (*T. h. grahamensis*), described by Allen (1895), is restricted to the highest elevations of the Pinaleño Mountains in southeast Arizona.

Description

A small, vocal squirrel, the chickaree is as often heard as seen. Adult-sized animals in Arizona generally range from just under 6 ounces to exceptional individuals of over 1 pound. Thirty-four individuals averaged 8.2 ounces, with little or no difference between males and females. Their total length is around 13 inches, ranging from under 12 inches to just over 14 inches.

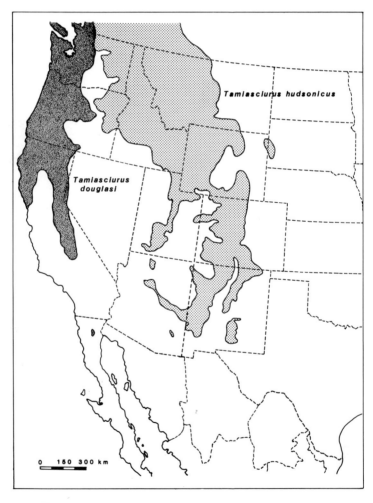

Figure 31. Distribution of *Tamiasciurus* in western North America.

Other distinguishing characteristics are short rounded ears and a flatter, less bushy tail that is measurably shorter than the length of the body. The winter coat of the Arizona chickaree is usually gray or olive-gray with a more or less rusty tinge. Like many other tree squirrels, the underparts are whitish and there is a distinct eyering. In summer and in juveniles, the appearance is more brownish and the bellies are often more gray than white. A black, or at least dark, lateral line usually separates the lighter belly from the darker upper parts. The reddish-orange fur is most pronounced along the center of the back, on the feet, and toward the base of a darkly tipped tail fringed in white.

There appears to be greater variation in color morphs than with other Arizona tree squirrels. One specimen (from the White Mountains) in the University of Arizona collection is coal black. Findley et al. (1975) found that animals from the San Mateo Range were darker than others from New Mexico, and Hoffmeister (1971) reported an albinistic individual that survived at least three summers on the North Kaibab.

From the specimens examined, few if any criteria distinguish the Graham Mountain spruce squirrel from its neighbors in the White Mountains. This is remarkable given the length of time that the low and arid Gila River Valley must have separated these populations.

Behavior. In addition to its diminutive size, the red squirrel is readily differentiated from other Arizona tree squirrels by its exaggerated movements and its vociferous scolding. The squirrel has a distinctive, perky or saucy manner, and its behavior is definitely "hyper" when compared to the actions of the tassel-eared squirrel. One's presence is announced and the squirrel's territorial rights are ascertained by a shrill *chr-r-r--che-e-e-e*, commonly given from a commanding tall conifer or snag. The squirrel's response to further intrusion may be either bold or shy; the animal may continue to scold and flick its tail, become or remain motionless, or scamper off to the thickest clump of branches in the highest tree available.

Food habits. Little is known about the food habits of red squirrels in Arizona. The species has an inherent predilection for coniferous seeds throughout its range, however (Layne 1954), and our animals are no exception. The squirrels are opportunists and take advantage of whatever cones their forest homes offer.

In late winter the terminal buds of spruce, fir, and other conifers are taken in addition to seeds from stored cones. If the winter is severe or stores are inadequate, the use of buds may be considerable even when suplemented by inner-bark and cambium. Their method of obtaining inner-bark is different from that of the Abert squirrels; bark is stripped away from large areas. Such feeding is also not confined to the terminal branches of ponderosa pines, although this species appears favored.

Male cones of several conifers are relished during the few weeks of spring that they are available. When present, these foods are superabundant and not stored or defended (Smith 1968). Shigo (1964) found red squirrels to also gnaw maples to obtain the early spring sap.

As summer progresses, branches of immature female cones are cut and the seeds eaten or the cones stored. Unlike the tassel-eared squirrel, which generally selects, cuts, and feeds on one cone at a time, the red squirrel often cuts a number of cones, letting them fall to the ground prior to storing or feeding on them. Falling cones are thus a good indicator of the squirrel's presence. False truffles and other fungi are also sought; those not eaten may be dried and stored. The subterranean forms are located by smell (Smith 1968). Animal food such as baby birds, insects, and carrion may be locally important in the diet when these items are available.

Conifer seeds are the staple, however, and cone cutting accelerates as the summer progresses. Species of particular importance in Arizona include white fir, subalpine fir, blue spruce, Engelmann spruce, white pine, ponderosa pine, and Douglas fir. From November through March, the only food available other than buds and inner bark is what the squirrel has stored.

Caches. Members of the genus *Tamiasciurus* are the only North American tree squirrels to store food in quantity. Food stores (caches) consist of heaps of unopened cones buried within piles of cone scale debris (middens) below a feeding perch. These sites invariably are in proximity to one or more large cone-bearing conifers and are usually at the base of a supporting structure such as a large-diameter tree or downed log (Vahle 1978; Fig. 32). Other favored storage sites are in hollow trees, against stumps, and in underground dens or crevices. One requirement is that caches be in shaded areas, depressions, or north-facing situations where moisture keeps the uncovered cones from opening (Flyger and Gates 1982). Middens may be 3 feet deep and 15 feet in diameter and represent the accumulated effort of several generations of squirrels.

Each squirrel has one primary cache that is vigorously defended against intruders—and for good reason; these stores are the squirrels' winter food supply and essential for the animal's survival. Although spruce and Douglas-fir cones provide the principal mainstay for red squirrels in Arizona, the cones of other conifers are also selected and may predominate in certain years and in certain locales. When available, fir cones appear to

Figure 32. Cone cache and midden of the red squirrel. (Photo by Robert Vahle.)

be favored above all others (Smith 1968). Fungi, too, are arranged on branches, dried, and stored in caches (Dice 1921, Cram 1924, Smith 1968). Later in the winter alder catkins may also be added to the cache (Smith 1968).

Nests. Both sexes make nests in tree cavities or construct them of conifer twigs, grass, leaves, and moss. Materials are carried to the site and wedged and interwoven with supporting branches to make a spherical bolus from 12 to 13 inches in diamter (Vahle 1978; Fig. 33). Nests are commonly in a dense Douglas-fir or spruce and are well fastened by twigs to a lateral branch near the main trunk (Bailey 1931). Vahle (1978) checked 232 bolus nests and four cavity nests and found most nests to be from 15 to 30 feet from the ground and generally on the south side of the trunk. Hoffmeister (1984) noted that the abandoned holes of woodpeckers provided most cavity nest sites.

The nests are lined with moss and grass. A hole in the side of the bolus leads to a snug cavity just large enough for the

Figure 33. Bolus nest of the red squirrel. (Photo by Robert Vahle.)

occupant to curl up comfortably (Bailey 1931). Most nests are within 20 feet of the primary cache, and most squirrels have more than one nest (Vahle 1978). The nest is a place to sleep, maintain body heat during winter storms, and raise the young. Food is never brought to the nest, and the young are only nursed here (Smith 1968). When a new nest is constructed — a common occurrence — dependent young are carried to their new home by their ventral parts; older young are sometimes coaxed to follow the mother to a new nest or one constructed for them (Smith 1968). Except for mothers with young, the nests are individual property and not shared with other squirrels.

Distribution

The little red squirrels, or chickarees, are everywhere creatures of cold climes and, although adaptable, are most abundant in mixtures of needle-leafed trees (Layne 1954, Smith 1968, Hall 1981). In the northern and western United States, *Tamiasciurus* is restricted to subalpine and cold temperate coniferous forests. As a consequence, they are confined in the Southwest to the highest elevations, reaching their southernmost limits in the subalpine forests of Arizona, New Mexico, and, in the case of the Douglas squirrel, Baja California Norte (Fig. 30). How this squirrel arrived and remained in the Sierra San Pedro Martir from the Sierra Nevadas without persisting in the relatively large subalpine forests of the San Gabriel, San Bernardino, and San Jacinto mountains in southern California is difficult to imagine.

Although often common within its range, the red squirrel in Arizona has a limited distribution. These squirrels are restricted to the larger mountain masses that possess subalpine conifer forests of spruce and fir—the North Kaibab Plateau, the Chuska and Lukachukai mountains on the Navajo Indian Reservation, Escudilla Mountain and the White Mountains, the Pinaleño Mountains, the San Francisco Peaks, and colder, wetter locales on the Mogollon Rim (Fig. 34).

Arizona red squirrels are rarely found much below 7,500 feet and are most often encountered above 8,300 feet. The small population on the Pinaleño (= Graham) Mountains occurs only

69

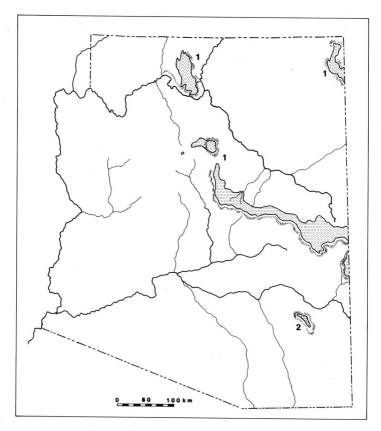

Figure 34. Distribution of red squirrels in Arizona.

on the highest peaks, mostly above 9,500 feet. The species'
upper limits are reached at timberline at around 11,000–11,600
feet in the San Francisco Peaks.

Red squirrels range from subalpine forest down through
mixed-conifer forest and are to be found, at least intermittently,
even in ponderosa pine forest. Apparently, however, they cannot exist in Arizona in mountains without well-developed
spruce-fir communities, and the squirrels are absent from the
cool forests of the Catalina, Huachuca, and Chiricahua mountains. Farther north the individual mountains are colder and not
so isolated, and these squirrels inhabit the spruce and fir clad
summits of Kendrick, Sitgreaves, Bill Williams, Bixby, and
Mormon mountains. They are absent, however, from the south

rim of the Grand Canyon and the Sierra Ancha, and Bradshaw mountains, which possess white firs and pine but lack subalpine fir (*Abies lasiocarpa*) and spruce.

Habitat. These squirrels require cold, moist, shaded conditions, and in Arizona favor mountain summits, chilly ravines, and forests adjacent to boggy flats. Precipitation can be expected to be between 25 and 35 inches, much of which falls as snow. The frost-free growing season is short—often less than 100 days—and winters are severe, with snow commonly covering the ground from November into May.

Like all tree squirrels, red squirrels prefer large, old trees in a closed setting. Older trees afford the best cone crops, and their interlocking canopies facilitate arboreal movement. Snags, piles and tangles of downed timber, and thickets of saplings enhance the forest for red squirrels. Conversely, the squirrels do less well in managed, even-aged forests and open forests of widely spaced trees are poor squirrel habitat.

The forest composition is extremely important. The most often used communities are subalpine forests of Englemann spruce (*Picea engelmanni*) and subalpine fir, and montane forests of Douglas fir and its associates—white fir, southwestern white pine, and ponderosa pine (Fig. 35). If other conifers are present, so much the better, and the transition area (ecotone) between these two boreal forests is especially productive for red squirrels. The greater the variety of cones to draw on, the better chance for a seed crop to get the squirrel through the winter.

Especially valuable, or at least frequented by the squirrels, are stands of blue spruce (*Picea pungens*) found in draws and along creeks, and the large cones of southwestern white pine, usually found at the forest edge on a windswept ridge or sunny slope. A more uncommon habitat is the bristle-cone pine (*Pinus aristata*)-limber pine (*P. flexilis*) community on the west slope of San Francisco Mountain.

At elevations below 7800–8000 feet, the montane forest becomes increasingly dominated by ponderosa pine, the density of red squirrels thins, and the animal becomes more and more restricted to mixed conifers along the cooler canyons and drainages. Before ponderosa pine gains total control of the landscape, the red squirrel has usually dropped out. An exception to this

71

Figure 35. Subalpine forest habitat of the red squirrel, North Kaibab, Kaibab National Forest, ca. 9,000 feet. The trees are Engelmann spruce, subalpine fir, and aspen.

was noted on the North Kaibab Plateau in 1971 when red squirrel populations were high and when a "bumper" ponderosa pine cone crop occurred. At that time the red squirrels descended into the ponderosa pine forest and set up territories to collect and store the bonanza. The squirrels were later forced to switch to other food sources and departed the pine forest to return to their more usual haunts. Analagous situations were noted by Rober Vahle (pers. comm.), who in some years, found caches of acorns associated with large Gambel oaks within ponderosa pine forest. The red squirrel is the most arboreal of Arizona's tree squirrels. Groups of large spruce, fir, and Douglas fir trees, close set, and with intersecting branches, are especially to the squirrel's liking, as they provide a reliable food source and escape cover. The more open pines are of less use, and red squirrels are rarely seen in aspens. Clear cuts and heavily logged forests are avoided. Nor is the squirrel to be looked for on the forest floor—where the tassel-eared squirrel is often sighted. Look—or, better yet, listen—for red squirels in the trees *above* the tangle of blowdowns and clutter of forest debris. Even when forced to the ground to collect and store his cones, the squirrel appears to prefer to scamper down fallen trees and scurry among the deadfalls rather than run across an open stretch of ground.

Vahle and Patton (1983) characterized red squirrel habitat on the Apache-Sitgreaves National Forest in the White Mountains. They found the highest squirrel concentrations in dense old growth of undisturbed stands containing groupings of trees of one or more dominant cone-bearing conifers 18 inches or more dbh. Douglas fir was the most common large tree. They found significantly more caches on uncut sites and on north and level exposures than on logged areas and on south-facing slopes. Cut plots had fewer trees per acre, a smaller average basal area (square feet of tree per acre), and fewer squirrels than unlogged plots. Caches on the cut sites were confined to groupings of trees left after overstory removal. Vahle and Patton recommended "group selection" as the best silvicultural method to preserve the multistoried character of red squirrel habitat and considered "even-aged" timber management less desirable for the squirrels.

Life History

There has never been a life history study of Arizona red squirrels. Consequently, most of the information on breeding behavior, reproduction, social habits, and mortality must be inferred from studies elsewhere. Fortunately, there have been a number of such investigations, and the biology of the animal is relatively well known.

Recruitment. Most female red squirrels come into heat (= estrus) in late winter or early spring—usually in late March or early April. Kemp and Keith (1970) suggested that these animals come into reproductive condition in response to feeding on spruce flower buds and that the number of young is related to coming food supplies. If so, they also follow behavior patterns similar to the fox and tassel-eared squirrels, the respective sexual activity of which is synchronized with the onset of deciduous tree and ponderosa pine flower emergence. Actually, a diet of any vitamin-rich food probably stimulates sexual development and the reproductive condition of the squirrels.

Although red squirrels usually have only one litter a year, two litters, one in the spring and one in the fall, have been reported in New York (Layne 1954). Not all females breed each year, and Smith (1968) found that in years of food shortage most *Tamiasciurus douglasi* females did not breed in the spring and none bred in the fall. Even in a good year, squirrels born the previous year don't breed until summer, as the animals don't attain sexual maturity until 10 to 12 months of age (Millar 1970).

Layne (1954) found that the reproductive season of red squirrels in New York lasts from January to October. Incomplete data for Arizona red squirrels suggest a shorter season, with breeding ending in July (Fig. 36). Females with embryos were collected in April and July, suggesting spring and summer breeding seasons, as reported by Layne (1954) in New York and Smith (1968) in British Columbia. Lactating females have been collected in Arizona up to August 6.

Like the tassel-eared and fox squirrels, the female is in estrus for only one day (Smith 1968). Cued by vaginal secretions, surrounding males are aware when she is receptive and are allowed to enter her territory the day she is in heat. One male establishes dominance, and a "mating chase" ensues. The female is closely pursued by this alpha male, who may stay with her for 5 hours or more, taking time off to repulse competitors. Fights are intense, and the combatants may be bloodied and scarred. During mating the female remains motionless on the ground or in a tree and, as the dominant male rarely has enough

74

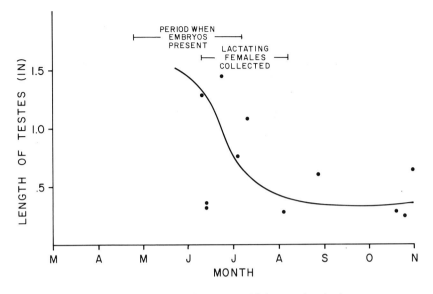

Figure 36. Known breeding season of Arizona red squirrels.

stamina to stay the day, she may mate promiscuously with several males (Smith 1968).

Gestation is 35 days (Ferron and Prescott 1977). During this time and the weaning period the female is particularly defensive toward other squirrels; the males have no parental duties and are excluded from the female's territory. From one to seven, pink, blind, and hairless young are born in the nest, where they remain for 45 days or more. Litter size depends on food sources and conditions but is usually between two and four.

Young squirrels first leave the nest tree when between seven and eight weeks old. It is now summer, and the young remain with their mother for only another two to three weeks. These half-grown squirrels are now weaned and set forth to establish their own territories.

Territories and home range. Each resident red squirrel has a defined territory that is defended against all others of the species. A squirrel without a territory is a vagrant; these animals are forced to make a living between the territories of other squirrels. Vagrants must establish a territory to protect their cache and survive the winter. Territory sizes depend upon the quality and quantity of food available and the density of the squirrel population.

A squirrel's territory is, in effect, his seasonal home range. Each territory normally consists of a reliable food source, a cache, a feeding perch and midden, one or more nests, and suitable escape cover (Vahle and Patton 1983). Territories are defended by vocal threats and the chasing off of intruders when necessary.

Vagrants occupy new territories by enlarging small undefended areas within another squirrel's range, by assuming the territory of a dead squirrel, or, less often, by assuming a territory through aggression and ritual chasing. The latter rarely occurs, because red squirrels recognize and respect the aggressive behavior of the defenders. The squirrels spend less than two percent of their time defending territories, and territorial disputes almost always go to the owner (Smith 1968).

Territories most often change owners in the spring. after winter mortality and when food supplies are more generally available. At that time some of the larger territories may be partitioned and shared. The tempo changes later in the year, when the possession of a cache makes the difference between perishing and survival. Even then, fights are rare, and almost never to the death. Smith (1968), who intensively studied the social organization of Douglas squirrels, found that the squirrels voluntarily left their respective territories only when: (a) a cone failure occurred, (b) food was more abundant on an adjacent, unoccupied territory, or (c) food became temporarily abundant in an otherwise vacant habitat. In these latter situations several squirrels may congregate prior to any attempt to establish new territories.

Young squirrels may be given part of the mother's territory. The mother may move the young to the edge of her territory where a nest has been provided, or she may shift the center of her territory to accommodate the youngster. Female young appear most likely to get these secondary areas, but in all cases the mother keeps the best territory for herself. Otherwise, the presence of young squirrels is tolerated only after appeasing calls are given, and only for a time (Smith 1968). Most young squirrels, particularly the males, become vagrants.

Population characteristics. As with some other sciurids, more males are taken from populations of red squirrels than females. Of 97 specimens in Arizona museum collections, 52, or 53%, are males. Layne (1954) found the sex ratios of adult red squirrels in New York to approximate 1:1 but that 60% of a collection of 147 juveniles were males. Smith (1968) hypothesized that greater mortality of juvenile males tended to equalize the sex ratio in older age populations and that males were actually predominant only in young populations.

Recruitment varies with the locality and year and is correlated with food supplies (Layne 1954, Smith 1968). Examination of the epiphyseal closure of the humerus in more than 100 Arizona red squirrels in 1970 showed that only 32% were young of the year, or 0.93 young per female, assuming a 1:1 sex ratio of adults. In 1971, a similar sized sample showed 53% to be young of the year (2.3 young per female; Brown 1972). Hunter success on this species increased 19% over this period, indicating an expanding population.

Red squirrel populations everywhere fluctuate by season and year (Flyger and Gates 1982). Squirrel foot collection boxes located on the Mogollon Rim southeast of Flagstaff showed an annual hunter success of from less than 0.1 to 0.33 squirrels per hunter during the years 1975 through 1980. During this period, red squirrels comprised from 3% to 19% of the squirrel harvest in this marginal red squirrel habitat (Table 6).

Densities. Although annual fluctuations in red squirrel populations are related to food supplies and reproductive success,

Table 6. Comparative Red Squirrel Hunt Information From Hunt Data Collection Boxes Southeast of Flagstaff, 1975–1981

	1975	1976	1977	1978	1979	1980	1981
Number of squirrel hunters reporting	101	249	380	406	182	88	186
Hunter days reported	162	376	520	541	262	124	240
Red squirrels bagged	9	66	71	59	60	4	14
Percent red squirrels in squirrel harvest	7	15	10	7	19	3	4
Red squirrels per hunter	0.09	0.27	0.19	0.15	0.33	0.05	0.04

sustained population levels depend on the quality of habitat. Because each primary cache represents the efforts of an individual squirrel, cache counts can be used to estimate the number of animals present (Vahle and Patton 1983). On this basis Vahle (1978) calculated a density in mixed conifer forest of about one squirrel per two acres on cutover south slopes to ca. one squirrel per acre on uncut level sites and north slopes during 1975–76—a "good" squirrel year. These densities in Arizona's White Mountains compare with Davis's (1969) reported densities of from 0.16 squirrel per acre in mixed jack pine (*Pinus banksiana*) and black spruce (*Picea mariana*) to 0.93 squirrel per acre in white spruce (*P. glauca*) forest in Canada. Layne (1954) reported densities up to and over one squirrel per acre in New York. Densities in poorer habitat and in poor squirrel years would, of course, be less. Overall densities of one squirrel per 5 acres can be considered "good populations" in good habitat.

Hoffmeister (1956) reported the Graham Mountain spruce squirrel (*T. h. grahamensis*) to be uncommon during his field work in the Pinaleño Mountains in 1951–52. He considered this race more silent and secretive than red squirrels in the White Mountains but thought the animal was more abundant prior to the introduction of Abert squirrels in the 1940s. Later, Minckley (1978) thought this race was extirpated, as he and others conducting a study of the vertebrates of the Pinaleño Mountains did not see any of these squirrels despite spending several weeks in the field each year from 1963 to 1967. They found Abert squirrels abundant and widespread, and Minckley suggested that this isolated race of red squirrel was an unsuccessful competitor with the introduced Abert squirrel.

The Graham Mountain spruce squirrel, however, was not extinct. I heard several during visits to the Pinaleños in the early 1970s, and Wildlife Manager Tom Waddell (pers. comm.) reported one taken by a hunter during the 1971 squirrel season. Nonetheless, the rarity of the squirrel was the subject of concern, and the Graham Mountain spruce squirrel was given protected status. Interest in the squirrel lagged.

On November 20, 1980, Tom Waddell, Rich and Patty Glinski, and I made a trip to High Peak to look for the squirrels. There, in pure Engelmann spruce forest, we collected a male and a female spruce squirrel and heard and photographed sev-

78

Figure 37. Englemann spruce forest home of the Graham Mountain spruce squirrel.

eral others (Fig. 37). The animals were not uncommon within this limited habitat, were vociferous, and appeared no more secretive than red squirrels elsewhere. Hoffmeister's and Minckley's concerns were not without foundation, however, as Layne (1954) noted that red squirrels in New York were unable to protect their caches from eastern gray squirrels where these species overlapped. The gray squirrel did not respect the territorial behavior of the red squirrel, and the gray's thievery of caches effectively excluded the red squirrel from gray squirrel habitat. It may well be that the introduced Abert squirrel now excludes the spruce squirrel from mixed conifer forest and any other habitats where ponderosa pine is present.

Mortality. Factors contributing to red squirrel mortality in Arizona are unknown. Halvorson and Engeman (1983) found survival curves of red squirrels on an island in Montana to be significantly related to high and low seed crop years. They and other investigators noted red squirrel populations to experience high juvenile mortality, a general leveling off of mortality after 36 months, and few individuals surviving past seven years. A significant difference in survival was found for males and females; mortality of young males was greater than that of females, but adult males survived at a greater rate than females.

Predation is rarely observed, and the red squirrel's principal enemy, the pine marten, is not found in Arizona. Goshawks certainly take some squirrels, and others wind up as road kills or are taken by hunters. Hunt pressure on this species is light, however, and the fate of vagrant and "surplus" red squirrels is largely unknown. The species is prone to a number of parasites and diseases, including tularemia and infectious viruses (Flyger and Gates 1982).

Management Importance

Because of their small size and limited distribution, red squirrels are not especially sought after by hunters. The proportion of Arizona's tree squirrel harvest that is made up of red squirrels can only be guessed at, but the animal's importance as game has probably been underrated. In mixed conifer and ponderosa pine dominated habitats along the Mogollon Rim, red squirrels constituted 17% of the harvest in 1969, 27% of the harvest in 1970, and 33% of the harvest in 1971. Even in primarily Abert squirrel country southeast of Flagstaff, red squirrels constituted from 3% to 19% of the bag between 1975 and 1981 (Table 6). A reasonable estimate would be that ca. 10% of the statewide tree squirrel harvest is red squirrels—between 4,000 and 10,000 animals per year for the years 1975–1981.

Foresters have complained that winter-feeding red squirrels damage conifers by nipping off terminal buds and retard forest regeneration by consuming up to 80% of the cone crop (Schmidt and Shearer 1971). These squirrels have also been reported to damage ponderosa pines by eating inner bark (Pike 1934). In some cases the entire cone crop of the forest may be collected and eaten (Finley 1969). Even in the best cone-production years, the squirrel selects cones with higher germination rates than those left on the trees (Wagg 1964). The squirrel stands accused of exerting "undue pressure" on forest regeneration.

These accusations appear overstated. Because red squirrel populations fluctuate, any pressures on forest regeneration are periodically relieved. Certainly, mixed conifer stands in the Sierra Ancha and Bradshaw mountains, where red squirrels are absent, show no more apparent regeneration of conifers than on mountains having the animal. It is not reasonable that an animal so dependent on its forest environment would evolve to reduce the extent and thrift of its home.

Because caches contain large numbers of fertile cones, foresters have raided them as a readily available seed source for conifer plantations. As with the tassel-eared squirrel, it is not the red squirrel, then, that reduces the forest, but the forester who threatens the squirrel, for if his cache is robbed the squirrel faces a winter without food stores. Forestry also thins and diminishes the squirrels' habitat, thereby reducing the squirrel population generally.

Summer home dwellers and visitors to the "high country" find the cheeky red squirrel an amusing neighbor, and spend many hours enjoying his antics. Should a personal acquaintance be desired, provide feeding stations of suet and a nest box at a convenient site. Boxes should be approximately 6" x 6" and 12" deep, with an entrance hole 1-¾" in diameter in an upper corner (Flyger and Gates 1982). The readily observed red squirrel is a welcome sight to hikers, hunters, picnickers, and fisherman—may he always grace our forests!

Squirrel Management

IN THE STRICTEST SENSE, wildlife management is the manipulation of animal numbers to achieve a projected purpose. To manipulate animal numbers upward (or downward) usually requires changing the carrying capacity of the featured animal's habitat. Such "active management" rarely is necessary to achieve a huntable surplus, as most wildlife populations at some time during the year are in excess of carrying capacity. A sizable number of these "excess" animals can normally be taken out of the population without affecting the next year's population level. Up to a certain level, the number of animals removed by hunting is usually from this "excess" and is compensatory to natural mortality. Keeping within this harvestable surplus is the object of most game management efforts, and squirrels are no exception. Present management efforts are to harvest squirrel numbers at a level that will be replenished naturally.

Management History

We now take squirrel seasons and squirrel hunting for granted. Such was not always the case. The game code adopted in 1912 when Arizona achieved statehood did not even mention squirrels. They had no status as game, and could be hunted anytime, anywhere, without restriction. Although the state game warden petitioned the Arizona legislature for a limited season on "pine squirrels" in 1927 and again in 1928, no action was taken, and tree squirrels remained without legal status. Then in 1928, after considerable effort by the Arizona Game Protective Association, Arizona voters passed a referendum to repeal the old game laws.

The year 1929 was a pivotal one for game management in Arizona. The Arizona Legislature responded to the referendum and the A.G.P.A. by sweeping away the old game code and enacting a new and progressive body of wildlife regulations. The most prominent feature of the "new game code" was the creation of an unpaid citizen Game and Fish Commission with authority to direct the work of the state game warden and adjust game regulations within certain limits set by law. Most game regulations could now be adjusted annually to respond to changing conditions without having to resort to the cumbersome task of revising the basic game laws.

The Game Code of 1929 gave complete protection to Kaibab and Chiricahua squirrels, and to all Arizona tree squirrels in that part of the state lying south of the Gila and Salt River baseline. The law further provided that a person may "take not to exceed six spruce [red] squirrels, Abert or tassel-eared gray squirrels (except Kaibab squirrels) in any one day between September 1, and October 31." Some confusion arose when the legislature authorized a squirrel season for 1929 of from October 1 through October 31, with a bag limit of "10 spruce or Abert's squirrels per day"!

The newly established Game and Fish Commission had the authority to shorten, alter, or reduce seasons and bag limits when commensurate with welfare of the game. The 1930 squirrel season was set to coincide with the general deer and turkey season opening in mid-October and continuing to November 15. This general arrangement remained in effect until 1935 when the commission curtailed the squirrel season for an indefinite period. Despite tree squirrels being favorite game animals, the season was closed because of an observed shortage of squirrels. Then, as now, Abert squirrel populations varied each year, but the effect of snow cover on squirrel populations wasn't known.

The winter of 1934–35 had been abnormally cold and long, with heavy snows, as was the winter of 1936–37. It was believed that a continued closed season would allow squirrel populations to "build up." Build up they did; the winters of 1937–38, 1938–39, and 1939–40 were exceptionally mild, with light snowfall. This resulted in "overpopulations" and a concern that the squirrels would damage the commercially valuable ponderosa pine forests. Populations were particularly dense on the Fort Valley Experimental Forest west of Flagstaff, and upon request of the U.S. Forest Service, the Arizona Game and Fish Department instituted a trapping and transplanting program to "relieve the forest" and increase squirrel distribution in the state (Lawson 1941). Between December 1, 1940, and January 24, 1941, 91 squirrels were trapped and distributed, as follows:

	Males	Females
Pinal Mountains	14	10
Granite Basin Recreation Area (Prescott)	4	4
Horsethief Basin Recreation Area (Bradshaw Mountains)	13	17
Santa Catalina Mountains (Summerhaven)	12	7
Ligon Game Farm Exchange		2
Dr. Dix; Experimental Station, Boise, Idaho	2	2
Dr. Koon; Experimental Station, Fairmont, West Virginia	2	2

The winter of 1940–41 was wet but warm. Squirrel populations continued to build, and in June 1941 the U.S. Forest Service expressed apprehension that severe damage was being done to the pines on Fort Valley Experiment Forest. The Forest Supervisor in Prescott also requested that no more releases of squirrels be made in Granite Basin because of possible damage to the limited stand of pines there.

This concern prompted the Arizona Game and Fish Department to have Leon Lawson conduct a special survey of the experimental forest and evaluate the state's squirrel habitat.

Using trapped and marked animals, Lawson (1941) conservatively estimated a squirrel population density on the Fort Valley reserve of one squirrel per six acres. Outside the reserve of mature forest, he also found good numbers of squirrels and estimated an overall density of about one-third that on Fort Valley Experiment Forest, or one squirrel per 20 acres. Lawson concluded that enough squirrels were present to justify a hunt, allowing two squirrels per day during the deer and turkey season. He and others questioned the desirability of a hunt, however, on aesthetic grounds, believing that most hunters would not want the squirrels molested. The commission postponed action and did not authorize a squirrel season in 1941.

Trapping was resumed on Fort Valley Experimental Forest on September 30, 1941, and continued through November 8, 1941. If anything, squirrels were more abundant than in 1940. One hundred ninety-three squirrels (100 males, 93 females) were trapped and released, as follows:

	Male	Female	Total
Pinal Mountains	19	15	34
Horsethief Basin	16	15	31
Catalina Mountains	19	21	40
Hualapai Mountains	15	22	37
Mt. Graham	29	20	49

Two males died during trapping and transplanting.

A limited squirrel season was declared by the commission for August 16 through November 15, 1942. Only Fort Valley Experimental Forest was open to hunting; the rest of the state remained closed. A stipulation of the declaration was that if an insufficient number of squirrels was removed during the hunt, additional measures to reduce the squirrel population would be authorized. The bag limit was set at five squirrels per day or in possession—rifles only.

In September, limited reconnaissance trips were made to the Pinal and Pinaleño (Graham) mountains to determine the fate of the transplants there (Arrington 1943). Although no squirrels were observed on these trips, the presence of clippings and other sign indicated that the transplants were taking hold.

The hunt of 1942 apparently had little effect on the squirrel population on Fort Valley Experimental Forest—the trapping program was resumed from January through May, 1943. The winter of 1942–43 had been dry and cold, and a long period of snow cover had been hard on the high population of squirrels. Trapped squirrels were in poor condition; many had mange, and trap mortality was high. Fifteen percent of the squirrels captured died, presumably from shock. Surviving animals were transplanted as follows:[2]

	Male	Female	Total
Pinal Mountains	23	19	42
Horsethief Basin	18	12	30
Hualapai Mountains	28	17	45
Mt. Graham	9	11	20

The commission was now convinced that a squirrel season was desirable. Accordingly, a season was authorized in 1943 and 1944 for the state's north zone deer hunt area (excluding Yavapai County). The dates of October 16 through November 15 were selected to coincide with the deer season. The bag limit was two squirrels per day or in possession.

Trapping and transplanting from the Fort Valley Experimental Forest continued. In May 1944, 30 squirrels were transplanted to Greer (where Abert squirrels were already present), 42 to Groom Creek in the Sierra Prieta near Prescott, four to Granite Dells near Prescott,[3] and 43 to the Hualapai Indian Reservation (Fraser Well area).

The winter of 1944–45 was one of great snowfall and severe cold. Because of the reduced population, only 31 squirrels were

2. The transplants to the Catalina Mountains had been discontinued at the request of Dr. Charles Vorhies at the University of Arizona. Vorhies feared possible hybridization with the native Catalina gray squirrel, four grays having been seen in pines at the release area near Summerhaven. He was too late. Reports of squirrel sightings and sign indicated that the transplant of Abert squirrels to the Catalinas was already successful (Arrington 1943).

3. These may have been the source of the Abert squirrels on Mingus Mountain. This population is known to be introduced, but no record of an introduction to Mingus Mountain can be found. Granite Dells does not possess much ponderosa pine, and the release site may have been on Mingus.

trapped; 29 were sent to the Hualapai Mountains and two to Greer. At the annual game season setting session, the commission voted to close the season on tree squirrels. The Abert squirrel was now too few in numbers and considered of more value as an aesthetic resource than as game. Besides, hadn't the low numbers followed two years of open seasons?

The season remained closed until 1950, when the commission authorized a short September season (from September 16 to September 30) in the Coconino and Sitgreaves National Forests—22 rimfire rifle or pistol only. The season was again closed in 1951, followed by a short open season during the first four days of the general deer season (October 24 to October 27) in 1952.

It wasn't until 1953 that an annual squirrel season was again established. That year the commission opened the squirrel season during the general deer season from October 23 to November 8 and included the Apache, Sitgreaves, and Coconino National Forests, the Bill Williams unit of the Kaibab National Forest, and the Mount Graham and Santa Catalina portions of the Coronado National Forest. The bag limit was five squirrels per day—rimfire rifles and pistols only. That year also marked the first time that survey and hunt data were collected. Although limited to a few hunter interviews, these reports indicated that Abert squirrels were considered palatable and that squirrel hunting was a potentially popular sport.

A similar season was set in 1954, and in 1955 parts of the Tonto and Prescott National Forests were opened to hunting. A field survey in 1953 resulted in only 33 squirrel hunters being checked. Squirrel hunters apparently constituted a very small percentage of the deer hunting public.

In 1958 a general squirrel season more similar to present arrangements was initiated. For the first time, squirrel hunters did not have to go afield when the deer hunt was in progress. Only the south zone (Graham and Catalina mountains) remained tied to the deer season for one more year. Shotguns were legalized, and the season was extended through November. With minor adjustments in the opening and closing dates, this general season has continued to the present. This framework has proved to be quite satisfactory; no species of squirrel is breeding at this time, no harm to the squirrel population has been demonstrated, and it is a good time to be in the woods. Squirrel hunting has since gained greatly in popularity, and since 1968 more than 10,000 hunters have annually taken to the field in search of squirrels (Fig. 38).

Success of the transplants. The trapping and stocking programs of the 1940s were an unqualified success in that huntable populations of Abert squirrels became established at all Arizona release sites, regardless of the size of the transplant. Today there are thriving populations in the Pinal, Bradshaw, Catalina, Pinaleño, Hualapai, and Mingus mountains as well as on the Hualapai Indian Reservation. The only limitations are the amount of pine forest available, and the squirrels have spread to all habitats within reach of their new homes. Some of the distances that the transplanted squirrels crossed to get to isolated pine stands are impressive.

By 1960, Abert squirrels had been sighted in the Rincon Mountains, and a well-established population is now found on Mica and Rincon peaks. These squirrels, unless released by persons unknown, had to cross a formidable barrier of chaparral and oak-grassland country to reach these limited pine forests from their transplant locales in the Catalinas.

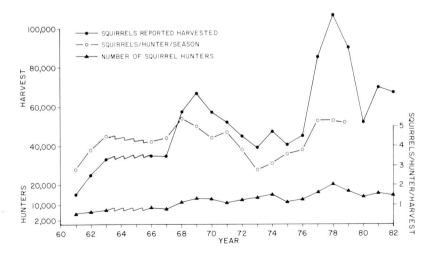

Figure 38. Number of squirrel hunters, squirrels harvested, and squirrels per hunter per season, 1960–1982.

The small areas of ponderosa pine in the Superstition Mountains now have Abert squirrels (Brown 1972). Presumably these are the result of dispersion from the introductions to the Pinal Mountains and the subsequent occupation of all suitable habitat there. Another possibility is that they arrived naturally from the San Carlos Indian Reservation through the Apache Mountains. Either way, they had to traverse many miles of chaparral and other unusable landscapes before finding suitable habitat.

In June 1980, Wildlife Manager Larry Voyles collected an adult male from a population of Abert squirrels on Juniper Mesa north of Camp Wood. This location is 75 airline miles from the nearest release site on Granite Mountain, with much of the intervening country unsuitable for Abert squirrels.

An increase in Abert squirrel range also appears to be taking place in native populations. In 1969 and 1970 I found Abert squirrel sign on Mazatzal Peak, Pine Mountain, and Mount Peale; Abert squirrels had not previously been reported from the Mazatzal Mountains. By 1980, Wildlife Technician Jim Wegge reported this species to be common farther south in the Mazatzals on Mount Ord, where I had earlier failed to find any evidence of them. It appears only a matter of time until Abert squirrels colonize Four Peaks and the pine stringers near Boulder Mountain—areas now occupied only by the Arizona gray squirrel.

Although Dr. Vorhies's fears of Abert squirrels inbreeding with Arizona gray squirrels was unfounded, it was probably unwise to have released Abert squirrels in the Bradshaw, Catalina, and Pinaleño mountains because of potential competition and displacement of native tree squirrels. For these reasons, Abert squirrels were *not* introduced to the Santa Rita, Huachuca, Chiricahua, and Pine mountains (Yavapai County), even though the pine forests in these ranges are no doubt suitable for them.

Attention now turned to the isolated stands of ponderosa pine on the Arizona Strip. These forests were without tree squirrels and, if suitable, would be logical release sites for transplanting the Kaibab race of tassel-eared squirrel, heretofore restricted to the Kaibab Plateau. In August and December 1965, Roland Kufeld, then Small Game Supervisor for the Arizona Game and Fish Department, conducted a reconnaissance of the Mt. Trumbull, Mt. Logan, Mt. Dellenbaugh, and Black Rock areas of the Arizona Strip to evaluate their suitability for a transplant. Kufeld (1966) thought these habitats questionable for tassel-eared squirrels but recommended a transplant to Mount Dellenbaugh as an experiment. The Kaibab squirrel was listed originally as a rare species in the *Red Book of Rare and Endangered Fish and Wildlife of the United States*. This, and the fact that Kufeld missed some of the better pine stands, prompted a renewed investigation of potential transplant sites. On November 10 and 11, 1971, the late Dr. D. I. Rasmussen and I surveyed the Mount Logan and Mount Trumbull areas, and later I evaluated pine forests in the Virgin Mountains, on Mt. Dellenbaugh, and on Black Rock. We found small but high quality pine habitats near Mt. Logan in the Sawmill Mountains and on Mt. Trumbull. A transplant of 20 to 40 Kaibab squirrels was recommended.

The winter of 1971–72 was severe, and only eight Kaibab squirrels, one male and seven females, were transplanted to Mt. Logan after 21 days of trapping effort. Three others died in transit. Four of the females were thought to be pregnant at the time of the release, and in May 1973 another male and a female were trapped and released. Three immatures were released the following fall, and postrelease investigations indicated that a Kaibab squirrel population was becoming established. Nonetheless, an additional eight Kaibab squirrels were trapped and released on Mt. Logan in 1977, the population on the Kaibab Plateau having recovered somewhat. Squirrels and their sign have been much in evidence ever since, and the animals have expanded their range to occupy Mt. Trumbull and Mt. Emma. Numerous sign and squirrels were noted in these areas in June 1983, and the area was opened to squirrel hunting in the fall of that year.

Present Management

The management of any species requires monitoring to determine if the population is increasing or decreasing. This calls for a census technique. To estimate the actual number of animals requires random sampling of the population and marking a sufficient number of individuals. The ratio of marked animals retrapped or recovered (killed) to unmarked animals provides a "Lincoln Index" or "Peterson Estimate" of the unmarked population (Seber 1973). However, one need not determine the total number of animals present to detect changes in population levels.

The number of squirrels seen in an area over a set period of time (time-area count), track counts, nest counts, and clipping counts have been used to index squirrel population levels (Brown 1982b). One of the best indices of animal abundance is hunter success. Given an adequate sample of hunters hunting enough animals over a sufficient time, the relative success of hunters at obtaining game should index the number of animals available. Allowing for the vagaries of weather, etc., it generally does, and this is the reason hunted populations are among the best understood.

Squirrel hunt success can be measured locally through data collection boxes located at strategic points in the forest (Fig. 39). If enough hunters are sampled and the same method and loca-

Figure 39. Squirrel hunt data collection box on the Mogollon Rim.

tions are used each year, hunting success can index year-to-year population changes. Hunt success information can also be obtained by sending a questionnaire to a sample of hunting license purchasers. Questionaires, however, cannot be used to determine species composition or gather age-ratio data. Both methods depend on the hunter for accurate data and are subject to response bias; i.e., there is a tendency for the more successful hunters to respond than those having poorer luck. The important thing to know is if hunt success (= population level) varies, and, if so, what factors might explain this variation.

Hunt success does vary. Begun in 1962, questionaires sent to a statistically valid sample of hunters indicated annual variation in the reported hunt success (Table 7). Hunter numbers and effort varied less than hunt success, and it appeared that squirrel populations fluctuate in response to factors other than hunting.

The effects of hunting. If hunting has a negative effect on population levels, hunt success and harvests should decline with

Table 7. Tree Squirrel Hunt Questionnaire Information, 1962–1982

Year	No. of Hunters[1]	No. of Days Hunted[1]	No. of Squirrels Reported[1]	Squirrels/ Hunter[2]	Squirrels/ Hunter/ Day[2]
1962	6,354	15,755	25,231	3.8	1.6
1963	7,270	15,742	33,352	4.5	2.1
1964	—	—	—	—	—
1965	—	—	—	—	—
1966	8,428	15,532	35,487	4.2	2.3
1967	7,930	19,978	35,241	4.4	1.8
1968	10,683	29,701	57,765	5.4	1.9
1969	13,349	36,408	66,950	5.0	1.8
1970	13,011	35,801	57,645	4.4	1.6
1971	11,235	34,112	52,340	4.7	1.5
1972	12,119	32,477	45,551	3.8	1.4
1973	13,882	32,470	39,290	2.8	1.2
1974	15,534	35,006	47,458	3.1	1.4
1975	11,271	26,891	40,736	3.6	1.5
1976	12,249	29,773	45,903	3.8	1.5
1977	16,216	42,378	85,508	5.3	2.0
1978	20,261	46,921	106,875	5.3	2.3
1979	17,337	52,011	90,367	5.2	1.7
1980	14,100	19,740	52,158	3.7	1.3
1981	15,911	47,733	69,864	4.4	1.5
1982	14,079	39,421	67,076	4.8	1.7

[1]Expanded.
[2]Does not consider reporting bias.

increasing hunt pressure. Conversely, populations in areas of declining hunt pressure or in areas closed to hunting (control areas) should experience population stability or an increase in squirrel numbers. If hunt pressure depresses squirrel numbers, an inverse relationship would be expected between the squirrel harvest and hunter numbers the previous year.

Just the opposite is true. Squirrel harvest numbers were positively related to the number of hunters ($r = 0.86$; $p \leq 0.01$), indicating that either the number of squirrels bagged is a function of the number of hunters afield, or hunter numbers are strongly influenced by the number of squirrels available.

In 1972, the clipping-count index on the unhunted Kaibab Plateau was about 1.6 times the count on the Mogollon Rim. Both indices decreased by more than 90% after long and heavy snow cover in 1972–73. The index on the hunted Mogollon Rim increased in 1974 and 1975 concomitant with light snow cover. The count on the Kaibab Plateau, subject to heavy snows, did not.

The relative differences between indices on the Kaibab Plateau and Mogollon Rim were supported by field observations. Although these data do not totally negate the effects of hunting on tassel-eared squirrel population levels, they indicate that, during the study, snow cover was the most important factor to affect tassel-eared squirrel population levels and that hunting did not prevent a population increase when snow cover was moderate.

Hunting, however, has been shown to reduce local populations of tree squirrels elsewhere, including species with a higher reproductive potential than Arizona squirrels (see e.g., Nixon et al. 1974). Obviously, hunting at some level will negatively affect squirrel numbers, at least locally. That level has yet to be determined for Arizona locales.

Collecting sex and age data. To obtain insight into factors governing animal population dynamics, data other than population trend must be collected. Foremost among these are information on age and sex. Together with population indices, sex and age ratios can provide measurements of recruitment, survival, and mortality.

Because tree squirrel sex ratios are close to 1:1, sex ratio information is usually not essential for population studies. Also, the only means of determining sex is examination of the sex organs, and examining large numbers of entire squirrels in the field is often impractical. The collection of sex organs is needed, however, for life history studies. Testes measurements provide outside dates for the breeding season, especially when the presence of sperm is documented. An even better indicator of male reproductive condition is the size of the bulbourethral and prostate glands, necessary for sperm delivery. Enlarged bulbourethral glands are a sure sign that the male is reproductively active (Fig. 40).

Knowledge of a female's reproductive status and history requires examination for embryos, placental scars, and evidence of lactation. Actual breeding condition is indicated by an enlarged cervix; these measurements can be used to determine the female's breeding season just as the bulbourethral measurements do for the male.

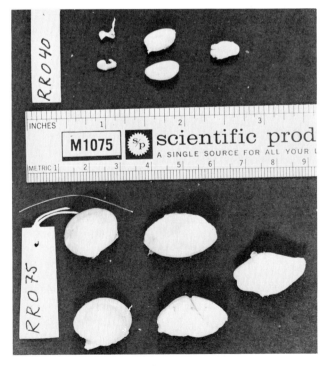

Figure 40. Sex organs (bulbourethral gland, prostate gland, and caudal epidymis) of a sexually inactive male Arizona gray squirrel *(above)* compared with those of a sexually active male collected in spring *(below)*.

Squirrels can be aged as juveniles (first-year animals) and adults (animals one year old and older). Methods include examination of the reproductive organs, calibrating dried eye lens weights, and noting the amount of closure of the epiphyseal cartilage on the humerus (Carson 1961). This last method is the most practical, as collected forelegs can be used to sample select populations.

Collected forelegs are mounted and X-rayed. Animals in which the epiphyseal cartilage is completely fused are judged to be adults; those having an "epiphyseal gap" are juveniles (Fig. 41). This technique was developed for eastern fox squirrels and gray squirrels but works well also for tassel-eared squirrels (Stephenson and Brown 1980). Tassel-eared squirrels have only one litter per year in midsummer, and there is less difficulty in determining fall ages for this species than for those that have

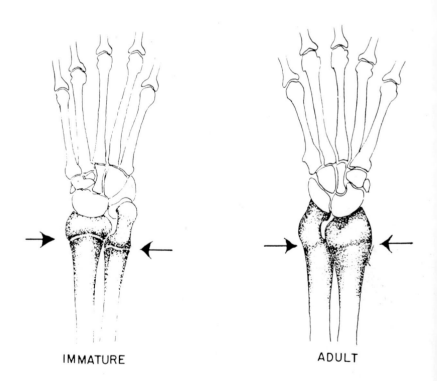

IMMATURE   ADULT

Figure 41. Epiphyseal cartilage of the foreleg of an immature and an adult squirrel.

more than one breeding season per year. Theobald (1983) also found the epiphyseal cartilage technique to be a good indicator of age in fall-winter collections of Arizona gray squirrels when compared to eye lens weights and reproductive condition. Squirrels cannot be aged by weight or pelage characters.

Factors influencing recruitment. Recruitment can be expressed as a ratio of the number of juvenile squirrels per adult, a ratio of the number of juvenile squirrels per adult female, or as the percentage of juveniles in the population. Because males may be more readily taken than females, and because sex ratios may vary annually and be influenced by differential mortality, young to adult ratios and percent young in the bag are probably the best measurements of recruitment. Still, squirrel sex ratios usually are close to 1:1, and the ratio of young to adult females provides a greater annual range in recruitment values. Experimentation with any or all of these means of expressing recruitment may therefore be called for.

Once a recruitment value is determined, and it can be shown that this rate varies annually, recruitment values can be compared with various environmental measurements (e.g., mast production, cone crops, precipitation, snowfall, etc.) to determine if any of these variables influence recruitment rate.

Factors influencing variations in recruitment rates of Arizona tree squirrels have yet to be resolved.

Survival and mortality rates. Given a method of indexing annual population levels and measuring annual recruitment rate, one can measure the rate of survival from one year to the next. An autumn population as indexed by squirrels per hunter in any given year represents the squirrels surviving from the previous year plus the annual recruitment. The ratio of adult squirrels per hunter to the number of adult and young squirrels per hunter the previous year is a measurement of the preceding year's survival. An estimated annual survival rate ($\hat{S}$) or the mortality rate reciprocal ($\hat{M} = \hat{S} - 1$) can then be calculated using the formula:

$$\hat{S} = \frac{\text{adult squirrels per hunter trip—present year}}{\text{all squirrels per hunter trip—previous year}}$$

Expressed algebraically, the formula would be: $\hat{S} = a_i/t_j$, where a_i = adult squirrels per hunter during the ith year, and t_j = total squirrels (adults and young) per hunter during the previous year.

These calculated survival rates can then be tested with any of several environmental factors, including hunt pressure, to determine variables that might influence mortality. Should a linear or multiple correlation coefficient show any of the factors tested to be significantly related to mortality, a measurement of the effect of that variable on the squirrel's welfare can be hypothesized. This value, when squared, approximates the amount of variation that could be explained by the event or events tested. Such calculations enabled Stephenson and Brown (1980) to ascertain that the number of days snow cover of four inches or more accounted for more than 70% ($r^2 = 0.72$) of the total annual mortality in tassel-eared squirrels in central Arizona.

Research Needs

Much remains to be learned about Arizona tree squirrels. The natural history and year-long food habits of our red squirrels have yet to be studied. The factors that determine Arizona gray squirrel abundance are unknown and we still do not know what level of hunt pressure on tassel-eared squirrels causes hunt mortality to become additive to natural mortality. There are other mysteries.

Knowing the fate of fall dispersed squirrels would be especially informative. What mechanisms cause females to colonize new territories? Are all colonists young animals? When Kaibab squirrels were introduced to the Sawmill Mountains, the populations rapidly expanded to densely occupy all available niches within 10 years. What would have happened to these pioneers had the "new habitat" already been occupied? Radio-telemetry should provide some answers to how young squirrels find a territory and what happens to those that do not.

Such natural history studies probably will be an unaffordable luxury, however. Current forest management practices dictate a need to determine the effects of logging on squirrel populations—particularly the tassel-eared and red squirrels.

Especially important is the need to know how much overstory removal squirrels in already naturally open forests can tolerate. The emphasis of current timber management prescriptions on taking out the older, best cone-producing trees is especially alarming. Shelterwood cuts, sanitary cuts, and the thinning of the forest below 80 square feet basal area feasibly could reduce squirrel population levels to token numbers and preclude these species as huntable game over large areas.

The only solution for multiple-use management appears to establish "leave," or deferred areas of "old growth" forest, within each timber sale. Determining the size and composition of such areas, as was initiated by Patton (1975) and Vahle and Patton (1983), is probably the most needed research. Although the tassel-eared and red squirrels are the species whose forests are most affected at present, future demands for hardwoods will soon affect our fox squirrels. The time to initiate such studies is now.

Squirrel Hunting

HUNTING SQUIRRELS IN THE SOUTHWEST always has been more sport than necessity. The Apaches, one of the few Indian tribes that resided in tree squirrel habitat, relegated squirrels as game for boys and considered squirrel hunting only as practice for larger quarry (Opler 1941). The Tarahumara Indians in the Sierra Madre took squirrel hunting a little more seriously. Their favored hunting technique, on flushing or locating a squirrel, was to cut down the tree containing the squirrel and have a hunting dog catch it on the ground (Lumholtz 1902:1:248–263)!

The first whites to report their squirrel hunting experiences in the Southwest were C. B. R. Kennerley and Heinrich Möllhausen, who accompanied the Whipple expedition of 1853–54 across northern Arizona. Möllhausen reported that a number of the men went squirrel hunting in the San Francisco Mountain area under conditions of bitter cold and deep snow. Then, as now, they found the animals secretive and only to be shot from the tops of tall trees. Although not many squirrels were bagged, they were a welcome addition to the camp fare (Davis 1982).

These hunter-collectors were followed by such enthusiastic sportsmen-naturalists as General George Crook and Dr. E. A. Mearns—transplanted squirrel hunters who started a southwestern squirrel hunting tradition that has continued to the present time.

Finding squirrels is easy—if they are out, active, and on the ground. When they are, all one has to do is stroll, or even drive, through likely looking habitat and watch for a bushy tail undulating through the woods. Squirrels are not always so vulnerable, however, and hunters must plan to increase their squirrel "encounters" if they are to be successful. This entails knowing squirrels and their habitat and employing a few proven hunting techniques.

Squirrels are not out every day, nor at all times of the day. Neither is there a particular time of day or period when they can always be counted on to be active. There are periods, however, when squirrels are not likely to be out. Squirrels usually hole up during stormy weather and appear to prefer clear, still days. Don't expect to see squirrels on windy days—these are anathema to them. Periods of driving rain or peristent snowfall are also stay-at-home days, although squirrels often are out on still, overcast days, even when an occasional light drizzle is in progress.

The time of day is important. From first light to mid-morning is the best time to look for squirrels, although on cold mornings the tassel-eared squirrels, especially, may wait for the sun to warm things up. Some squirrels usually are active until noon, with lesser numbers seen through the afternoon. Unlike some other wildlife, squirrels are not particularly busy in the late afternoon, and the last two hours before dark may be "dead time."

An especially good bet is the first quiet day following several days of inclement weather. The squirrels are hungry and make up for their forced inactivity by being especially active. A fresh snowfall can also help in locating animals. Newly made tracks, husked cones, and fallen clippings are give-aways; the maker of such "sign" can usually be found with the aid of binoculars.

Some hunters, upon seeing a squirrel foraging on the ground, immediately rush toward the animal, forcing it to take to the nearest tree. The squirrel is then shot before it can get out of sight. Although this may be an effective method when hunting out of a vehicle or when hiking, experienced hunters prefer a more stealthy approach.

Pussyfooting through the forest, using ears as well as eyes, watch for sign; look for the silhouette of a tail or pair of ears, or try to catch a white eye-ring among the foliage. Especially listen for feeding squirrels to betray themselves: a dropped cone, a far-off warning bark, a rustling through the trees are tip-offs to a squirrel's presence. Most squirrels are bagged when spotted frozen in an exposed position or "caught out" as they scurry to a safer tree.

Most successful are the still hunters—a technique requiring more patience than I can usually muster. This method consists of stalking through likely looking habitat (a prime requisite for any technique) and looking for fresh sign. Once evidence of recent squirrel activity is located, the hunter finds a comfortable spot and waits for a squirrel to show itself. This may take some time, as alerted squirrels remain motionless for almost an hour. Those not startled soon return to their business, however, and the hunter will eventually be rewarded by the sounds of resumed feeding. Good hunters spend from 30 minutes to an hour on a stand, using binoculars and listening.

Once glimpsed, the squirrel has lost his first line of defense. His only chance now is to move out quickly, to get out of sight in foliage as high and as dense as possible. Here he will flatten himself against a large limb, remain absolutely motionless, and lie "doggo." He's good at this, and both tassel-eared and gray squirrels use this escape technique effectively.

Hollow snags and holes are scarce in Arizona and sometimes a squirrel will retreat to his nest. Once inside, as in other dense foliage, he is almost impossible to see. Remember that a sportsman never shoots into a nest; this only results in dead or wounded squirrels that cannot be retrieved.

A word about choice of weapons: although both shotguns and rifles are legal for taking squirrels, the .22 rifle was made for squirrel hunting. Most of the many squirrels I have shot in Arizona were collected as specimens for study and taken with a shotgun. However, there is little marksmanship to be had in bagging squirrels in this fashion. On the contrary, a well-placed chest or head shot with a scope-sighted .22 can still thrill the boy or girl in any of us. And, after all, tree squirrels are primarily game for the youngster—whether 16 or considerably older.

For some reason, Arizona tree squirrels have a reputation for tasting "piney." This may be true of animals that have spent considerable time feeding on inner bark, but I have always found tree squirrels to be fine table fare. Properly cared for and prepared, squirrel is the culinary equal of cottontail or quail.

For the best eating, clean squirrels immediately after killing. Skin the animal first—a good fast method is to cut the skin behind the shoulders and pull both ways. Old squirrels are much tougher to skin then young ones. Once the legs are freed, the feet, head, and tail can be cut off. Eviscerate the carcass by grasping the squirrel's forefeet in the left hand and its hind feet in your right; snap the slit belly or ventral portion of the squirrel away from you.

At first opportunity wash the carcass thoroughly and keep it cool. Cut the squirrel into quarters and soak it overnight in salt water or marinate it. Grilled, fried, or slow-cooked in a stew, you'll find haunch of squirrel a delectable treat.

Bibliography and Literature Cited

Allen, J. A. 1893. List of mammals and birds collected in northeastern Sonora and northwestern Chihuahua, Mexico, on the Lumholtz archaeological expedition, 1890–92. Bull. Amer. Mus. Nat. Hist. 5:27–42.

Allen, J. A. 1894. New North American mammals. Bull. Amer. Mus. Nat. Hist. 6:349–350.

Allen, J. A. 1895. Mammals from Arizona and Mexico. Bull. Amer. Mus. Nat. Hist. 7:244–255.

Arrington, O. N. 1943. Completion report—Abert squirrel. Arizona Game and Fish Comm. Proj. 11-D:1–23.

Axelrod, D.I. 1979. Age and origin of Sonoran Desert vegetation. Calif. Acad. Sci. Occas. Pap. 132:1–74.

Bailey, V. 1931. Mammals of New Mexico. USDA, Bur. Biol. Surv. North Amer. Fauna 53:1–412.

Brown, D. E. 1971. Reevaluation of the Mount Logan and Mount Trumbull areas as potential Kaibab squirrel habitat. Arizona Game and Fish Dept. Special Rept. W-53-R-21:1–5.

Brown, D. E. 1972. Tree squirrel management information. Arizona Game and Fish Dept. Progress Rept. W-53-R-22:1–5.

Brown, D. E., ed. 1982a. The biotic communities of the American Southwest—United States and Mexico. Desert Plants 4(1–4):1–342.

Brown, D. E., 1982b. The use of "clippings" to index tassel-eared squirrel population levels. J. Wildl. Manage. 46:520–525.

Bryant, M. D. 1945. Phylogeny of nearctic sciuridae. The Amer. Midl. Nat. 33:255–390.

Burt, W. H. 1933. Mammals of southern Arizona. J. Mammal. 14:114–122.

Cahalane, V. H. 1939. Mammals of the Chiricahua Mountains, Cochise County, Arizona. J. Mammal. 20:418–440.

Caire, W. 1978. The distribution and zoogeography of the mammals of Sonora, Mexico. Ph.D. Diss., Univ. of New Mexico, Albuquerque. Vol. 1:1–343.

Carson, J. D. 1961. Epiphyseal cartilage as an age indicator in fox and gray squirrels. J. Wildl. Manage. 25:90–93.

Cockrum, E. L. 1960. The recent mammals of Arizona, their taxonomy and distribution. Univ. of Ariz. Press, Tucson. 276 p.

Coues, E. 1867. The quadrupeds of Arizona. Amer. Nat. 1 (August, September, October, December):281–292, 351–363, 393–400, 531–541.

Coughlin, L. E. 1938. The case against the tuft-eared squirrel. USDA For. Serv., Rocky Mt. Res. Bull. 21- 10–12.

Cram, W. E. 1924. The red squirrel. J. Mammal. 5:37–41.

Davis, D. W. 1969. The behavior and population dynamics of the red squirrel, *Tamiasciurus hudsonicus*, in Saskatchewan. Ph.D. Diss., Univ. Arkansas, Fayetteville. 222 p.

Davis, G. P. 1982. Man and wildlife in Arizona: the American exploration period, 1824–1865. N. B. Carmony and D. E. Brown, eds. Ariz. Game and Fish Dept., Phoenix. 232 p.

Dice, L. R. 1921. Notes on the mammals of interior Alaska. J. Mammal. 2:20–28.

Doutt, J. K. 1931. A new subspecies of the Arizona gray squirrel (*Sciurus arizonensis* Coues). Ann. Carnegie Mus. 20:271–273.

Farentinos, R. C. 1972a. Observations on the ecology of the tassel-eared squirrel. J. Wild. Manage. 36:1234–1239.

Farentinos, R. C. 1972b. Social dominance and mating activity in the tassel-eared squirrel (*Sciurus aberti ferreus*). Anim. Behav. 20:316–326.

Farentinos, R. C. 1972c. Nests of the tassel-eared squirrel. 1972. J. Mammal. 53(4):900–903.

Farentinos, R. C. 1974. Social communication of the tassel-eared squirrel (*Sciurus aberti*): a descriptive analysis. Z. Tierpsychol. 34:441–458.

Farentinos, R. C. 1979. Seasonal changes in home range size of tassel-eared squirrels (*Sciurus aberti*). Southwest. Nat. 24:49–62.

Farentinos, R. C., P. J. Capretta, R. E. Kepner, and V. M. Littlefield. 1981. Selective herbivory in tassel-eared squirrels: role of monoterpenes in ponderosa pines chosen as feeding trees. Science 213:1273–1275.

Ferron, J., and J. Prescott. 1977. Gestation, litter size, and number of litters of the red squirrel (*Tamiasciurus hudsonicus*) in Quebec. Can. Field Nat. 91:83–84.

Ffolliot, P. F., and D. R. Patton. 1978. Abert squirrel use of ponderosa pine as feed trees. USDA For. Serv. Res. Note RM-362:1–4.

Findley, J. S., A. H. Harris, D. E. Wilson, and C. Jones. 1975. Mammals of New Mexico. Univ. Of New Mexico Press, Albuquerque. 360 p.

Finley, R. B., Jr. 1969. Cone caches and middens of *Tamiasciurus* in the Rocky Mountain region. Univ. of Kansas Mus. Nat. His. Misc. Publ. 51:233–273.

Flyger, V., and J. E. Gates. 1982. Pine squirrels. pp. 230–238 *In* J. A. Chapman and G. A. Feldhamer, Wild mammals of North America. Johns Hopkins Univ. Press, Baltimore and London, 1147 p.

Goldman, E. A. 1928. The Kaibab or white-tailed squirrel. J. Mammal. 9:127–129.

Goldman, E. A. 1931a. *Sciurus aberti chuscensis* Goldman. Proc. Biol. Soc. Washington 44:133.

Goldman, E. A. 1931b. Three new rodents from Arizona and New Mexico. Proc. Biol. Soc. Wash. 44:133–136.

Goldman, E. A. 1933a. Five new rodents from Arizona and New Mexico. Proc. Biol. Soc. Wash. 46:71–77.

Goldman, E. A. 1933b. New mammals from Arizona, New Mexico, and Colorado. J. Wash. Acad. Sci. 23:463–473.

Golightly, R. T., Jr., and R. D. Ohmart. 1978. Heterothermy in free-ranging Abert's squirrels (*Sciurus aberti*). Ecol. 59:897–909.

Hall, E. R. 1981. The mammals of North America. 2nd ed., Vol. 1. John Wiley & Sons, New York, Chichester, Brisbane, Toronto. 600 p.

Hall, J. G. 1981. A field study of the Kaibab squirel in Grand Canyon National Park. Wildl. Monogr. 75:1–54.

Halvorson, C. H., and R. M. Engeman. 1983. Survival analysis for a red squirrel population. J. Mammal. 64:332–336.

Hobbs, D. E. 1980. The effects of habitat sound properties on alarm calling behavior in two species of tree squirrels. Ph. D. Diss., Univ. of Arizona, Tucson.

Hoffmeister, D. F. 1956. Mammals of the Graham (Pinaleño) Mountains, Arizona. Amer. Midland Nat. 55:257–288.

Hoffmeister, D. F. 1971. Mammals of Grand Canyon. Univ. of Illinois Press, Urbana, Chicago, London. 183 p.

Hoffmeister, D. F. [1985] In press. Mammals of Arizona. Univ. of Ariz. Press, Tucson.

Hoffmeister, D. F., and V. E. Diersing. 1978. Review of the tassel-eared squirrels of the subgenus Otosciurus. J. Mammal. 59:402–413.

Hungerford, C. R. 1964. Vitamin A and productivity in Gambel's quail. J. Wildl. Manage. 28:141–147.

Keith, J. O. 1965. The Abert squirrel and its dependence on ponderosa pine. Ecol. 46(1 and 2):150–163.

Kemp, G. A., and L. B. Keith. 1970. Dynamics an regulation of red squirrel (Tamiasciurus hudsonicus) populations. Ecology 51:763–779.

Kufeld, R. C. 1966. Tree squirrel management information. Arizona Game and Fish Dept. Completion Rept. W-53-R-16:1–5.

Larson, M. M., and G. H. Schubert. 1970. Cone crops of ponderosa pine in central Arizona, including the influence of Abert squirels. USDA For. Serv. Res. Pap. RM-58. 15 p.

Lawson, L. 1941. Survey of Abert squirrel populations in the state, June 13, 1941 to June 19, 1941. Proj. 11-D. Ariz. Game & Fish Dept., Phoenix. 3 p.

Layne, J. N. 1954. The biology of the red squirrel, Tamiasciurus hudsonicus loquax (Bangs), in central New York. Ecol. Mongr. 24:227–267.

Lee, M.R., and D. F. Hoffmeister. 1963. Status of certain fox squirrels in Mexico and Arizona. Proc. Biol. Soc. Wash. 76:181–190.

Leopold, A. S. 1959. Wildlife of Mexico: the game birds and mammals. Univ. Calif. Press, Berkeley. 568 p.

Ligon, J. S. 1927. Wildlife of New Mexico: its conservation and management. New Mexico Dept. of Game and Fish, Santa Fe. 212 p.

Lindsay, E. H., and N. T. Tessman. 1974. Cenozoic vertebrate localities and faunas in Arizona. Ariz. Acad. Sci. 9:3–24.

Lumholtz, C. 1902. Unknown Mexico. Charles Scribner's Sons, New York. 1:1–530, 2:1–496.

Madson, J. 1964. Gray and fox squirrels. Olin Mathieson Chemical Corp., East Alton, Ill. 112 p.

Martin, P. S. 1970. The last 10,000 years. The University of Arizona Press, Tucson. 87 p.

Maser, C., J. M. Trappe, and R. A. Nussbaum. 1978. Fungal-small mammal interrelationships with emphasis on Oregon coniferous forests. Ecology 59:799–809.

Maser, C., J. M. Trappe, and D. C. Ure. 1978. Implications of small mammal mycophagy to the management of western coniferous forests. Trans. North Amer. Wildl. and Natur. Resour. Conf. 43:78–88. Wildl. Manage. Instit.

McKee, E. D. 1941. Distribution of the tassel-eared squirrels. Plateau 14:12–20.

Mearns, E. A. 1907. Mammals of the Mexican boundary of the United States. Part 1. U.S. Nat. Mus. Bull. 56:1–530.

Merriam, C. H. 1904a. Two new squirrels of the Abert group. Bio. Soc. Wash. Proc. 17:129–130.

Merriam, C. H. 1904b. Two new squirrels of the *aberti* group. Proc. Biol. Soc. Wash. 18:163–166.

Millar, J. S. 1970. The breeding season and reproductive cycle of the western red squirrel. Can. J. Zool. 48: 471–473.

Minckley, W. L. 1968. Possible extirpation of the spruce squirrel from the Pinaleño (Graham) Mountains, south-central Arizona. J. Ariz. Acad. Sci. 5:110.

Monson, G. 1972. Unique birds and mammals of the Coronado National Forest. USDA, Forest Service. U.S. Gov. Print. Office. pp. 64–66.

Nixon, C. M., R. W. Donohoe, and T. Nash. 1974. Overharvest of fox squirrels from two woodlots in western Ohio. J. Wildl. Manage. 38:67–80.

Opler, M. E. 1941. An Apache life-way. Univ. of Chicago Press. 500 p.

Patton, D. R. 1974. Estimating food consumption from twigs clipped by the Abert squirrel. USDA For. Serv. Res. Note RM-272:1–3.

Patton, D. R. 1975a. Abert squirrel cover requirements in southwestern ponderosa pine. USDA For. Serv. Res. Note RM-145:1–12.

Patton, D. R. 1975b. Nest use and home range of three Abert squirrels as determined by radio tracking. USDA For. Serv. Res. Note RM-281:1–3.

Patton, D. R. 1977. Managing Southwestern ponderosa pine for the Abert squirrel. J. Forest. 75.

Patton, D. R., H. G. Hudak, and T. D. Ratcliff. 1976. Trapping, anesthetizing, and marking the Abert Squirrel. USDA For. Serv. Res. Note RM-307:1–2.

Patton, D. R., T. D. Ratcliff, and K. J. Rogers. 1976. Weight and temperature of the Abert and Kaibab squirrels. Southwest. Nat. 21:235–238.

Pearson, G. A. 1950. Management of ponderosa pine in the Southwest. USDA, Agr. Monogr. 6:1–218.

Pederson, J. C., R. N. Hasenyager, and A. W. Heggen. 1976. Habitat requirements of the Abert squirrel (Sciurus aberti navajo) on the Monticello District, Manti-LaSal National Forest. Utah State Div. Wildl. Res. Publ. 76-9:108 p.

Pederson, J. C., and A. L. Pederson. 1976. Tassel-eared squirrels of North America: a bibliography. Utah State Div. Wildl. Res. Publ. 76-14:22 p.

Pike, G. W. 1934. Girdling of ponderosa pine by squirrels. J. For. 32:98–99.

Ramey, C. A., and D. J. Nash. 1976. Coat polymorphism of Abert's squirrel, Sciurus aberti, in Colorado. Southwest. Nat. 21:209–217.

Rasmussen, D. I. 1941. Biotic communities of Kaibab Plateau, Arizona. Ecol. Monog. 11:229–275.

Rasmussen, D. I. 1972. National and international interest in the Kaibab squirrel: a problem analysis. 91 p. Unpublished report prepared by Region 3, USDA For. Serv., Albuquerque, N.M., on file at Rocky Mtn. For. and Range Exp. Stn., Tempe, Arizona.

Rasmussen, D. I., D. E. Brown, and D. Jones. 1975. Use of ponderosa pine by tassel-eared squirrels and a key to determine evidence of their use from that of red squirrels and porcupines. Ariz. Game & Fish Dept. Wildl. Digest 10:1–12.

Ratcliff, T. D., D. R. Patton, and P. F. Ffolliott. 1975. Ponderosa pine basal area and the Kaibab squirrel. J. Forest. 73:284–286.

Reynolds, H. G. 1963. Western goshawk takes Abert squirrel in Arizona. J. For. 61:839.

Schmidt, W. C., and R. C. Shearer. 1971. Ponderosa pine seed: for animals or trees. U.S. For. Serv. Res. Pap. INT-112:1–14.

Seber, G. A. F. 1973. The estimation of animal abundance and related parameters. Hafner Press, New York. 506 p.

Shigo, A. L. 1964. A canker on maple caused by fungi infecting wounds made by the red squirrel. Plant Dis. Rept. 48:794–796.

Simpson, G. G. 1945. Principles of animal taxonomy. Columbia Univ. Press, New York. 247 p.

Smith, C. C. 1968. The adaptive nature of social organization in genus of three squirrels *Tamiasciurus*. Ecol. Monogr. 33:31–63.

Smith, C. C. 1981. The indivisible niche or *Tamiasciurus*: an example of nonpartitioning of resources. Ecol. Monogr. 51:343–363.

Stephenson, R. L. 1975. Reproductive biology and food habits of Abert's squirrels in central Arizona. M.S. Thesis, Ariz. State Univ. 66 p.

Stephenson, R. L. and D. E. Brown. 1980. Snow cover as a factor influencing mortality of Abert's squirrels. J. Wildl. Manage. 44:951–955.

Theobald, D. U. 1983. Studies on the biology and habitat of the Arizona gray squirrel. M.S. Thesis, Arizona State Univ.

Trowbridge, A. H., and L. L. Lawson. 1942. Abert squirrel-ponderosa pine relationships at the Fort Valley Experimental Forest, Flagstaff, Arizona. Ariz. Coop. Wildl. Res. Unit., Tucson. 38 p.

Vahle, J. R. 1978. Red squirrel use of southwestern mixed coniferous habitat. M.S. Thesis, Arizona State Univ. 100 p.

Vahle, J. R., and D. R. Patton. 1983. Red squirrel cover requirements in Arizona mixed conifer forests. J. Forest. Jan. 14–15, 22.

Wagg, J. W. B. 1964. Viability of white spruce seed from squirrel-cut cones. For. Chron. 40:98–110.

Yoder, R. G. 1958. The Chiricahua fox squirrel. Mammalogy project report. Univ. of Ariz. 15 p. mimeo.

Glossary

Allopatric: Not overlapping; separated.

Alpha Male: Dominant male; the lead male in a mating chase.

Bolus: Round or ball-shaped; ball-shaped nest.

Boreal: Northern.

Cache: Stored food.

Cervix: Distal sphincter of uterus; birth canal.

Compensatory Mortality: The number of animals lost or taken from a population that would be lost later in the year from natural causes.

Conelets: Unfertilized female or ovulate cones; stroboli.

Consociations: Pure stands; plant communities essentially dominated by one species.

Conspecific: The same species.

Disjunct: Separated; unconnected.

Diurnal: Active during daylight hours.

Dorsal: The back or upper parts.

Drey: The leaf nest of a squirrel.

Ecotone: The junction of different habitats; the area where habitats overlap or where one habitat phases into another.

Endemic: Native, not introduced.

Epiphysis: The fore end of the long bone that ossifies separately and later becomes fused to the main shaft of the bone.

Estrus: Period of female fertility; period of sexual acceptancy by the female.

Geoflora: The collective plant life (= flora) of a particular geologic time or age.

Mast: The harvest of wild fruits and nuts; acorns, berries, etc.

Mesic: Wet; relatively damp habitats.

Midden: Debris left from feeding in a select area; e.g., cone scales.

Monoecious: Plant having both sexes in the same individual.

Monomorphic: One form; used to describe animals that have similar-appearing sexes.

Rostrum: Bony part of the snout.

Sclerophyll: hard leaved; leaves with a waxy, or otherwise drought-resistant coating.

Staminate: Pollen; male flowers.

Stroboli: First-year conelets.

Sympatric: Overlapping; having shared ranges.

Ventral: Underside.

Xeric: Dry; relatively arid habitats.

61140068

Designed by Harrison Shaffer
Type composed by Tucson Typographic Service, Inc.
Color separations by American Color Corp.
Printed by Fabe Litho, Ltd., Tucson, Arizona

9544